The Shadows
Lifted from Death

The Shadows Lifted from Death

**As given through
A. H. BURBIDGE**

London 2011

Roundtable
Publishing Limited

The First Edition was published by Henry Burbidge and Harold Swansborough, being the executors of the late A. H. Burbidge.

The Second Edition was published in CD-ROM by the Allan Kardec Publishing Ltd – 2001. The copyright for this edition were kindly conceded to the AKP Ltd by the executors, Henry Burbidge and Harold Swansborough.

The Third Edition -
Copyright © 2010 by
ROUNDTABLE PUBLISHING LTD

ISBN 978-0-9564493-4-4

Editing and Introduction by Janet Duncan

Cover design and layout by Rones José Silvano Lima

Edition of
ROUNDTABLE PUBLISHING LTD
London-UK
roundtable.uk@gmail.com
www.roundtablepublishing-uk.com

Acknowledgments

Both the Editor and Publisher wish to thank Mr. and Mrs. Norris and Mr. Swansborough for their permission to publish this valuable material received from the World of Spirit.

Contents

PART II

Preface

Augustus Henry (Harry) Burbidge was born on 10th September 1891 at Watford, later moving to the Portobello Road, in Central London. As a young man he worked as a shop assistant in a department store, where he met Catherine Slater, also working at the same store.

In November of 1912 Harry joined the Metropolitan Police Force as a Constable in the Kingston-upon Thames area in Surrey. He continued to see Catherine Slater and they were married on 26th December 1913. At the outbreak of the Great War in 1914 Harry was transferred to the Criminal Investigations Department and was moved to Clapham, then to Kings Cross and again to Wood Green, all within the Metropolitan area of London.

Over the years the couple had four children, two girls and two boys. Harry eventually retired from the Police Force in 1935 and received a Certificate for Exemplary Conduct during service. He then joined the Tottenham Borough Council and at the outbreak of the Second World War in 1939 he was made Chief A.R.P. Warden. At this time his family were evacuated to Dawlish in Devon. Later on when the bombing became too bad in Tottenham he was persuaded to join them in Dawlish.

His experiences in the Police Force and during the war caused him to explore the possibility of an existence beyond the physical plane. His wife developed as a medium and so together they used their house in Dawlish as a Spiritual and Healing

Sanctuary. In the evenings Harry would frequently meditate alone in a room dedicated to spiritual purposes, and it was there, during this period, that he was controlled and wrote this book.

Eventually the Dawlish Spiritualist Church was opened in 1954, when Harry Burbidge became the Founder President and his wife the Vice President.

His family have studied the writings and confirm that the thoughts are not those of their father, but those of an unknown entity. They consider them worthy of a wider audience than just themselves. They believe them to be good evidence of life beyond this physical plane.

We find that several members of Harry's family became spiritually minded. As a matter of interest Harry's eldest son, Henry, also served in the Metropolitan Police Force. He too joined a Spiritualist Church in Lewisham and served as a Committee Member, Secretary and finally as President. His wife Kathleen was also on the Committee as Mediums Secretary. When Harry's youngest son passed to spirit in 1984 his wife Fay became interested in Spiritualism and is now a known Healer and Medium.

Augustus Henry (Harry) Burbidge
1891 - 1963

Introduction

Having come into our hands unexpectedly and obviously not by coincidence, we have great pleasure in presenting this small book to the public. It may be small in size, but we feel it is large in the sense of opening up vast areas for thought and meditation, and most especially of taking away any fear that death is the end of existence. Rather it confirms yet again that Life is continuous, that we are immortal Beings, and that death does not exist.

As we look about us, especially in Nature, we see a constancy of renewal. Even in the act of disintegration we see and understand the process of a decaying element returning to the point of origin to be re-cycled. How could it be otherwise? Nothing in Nature is wasted, even excrements become a valuable fertiliser for the plant kingdom, so it may flourish and in turn give us the many products that we require for our daily existence.

The spiritual beliefs, namely Spiritualism and Spiritism, both teach survival as being part of the Laws of Nature. But what of the after life? Do we still cling to the image of a fluffy white cloud, where we sit and play a harp? Surely not! Can we not go a step further and understand that Life has a continuous sequence? So then, what comes after the so called death?

This book is the experience of one person in the afterlife. This may not be convincing for some, who continue to demand endless proof. Nevertheless, it is in fact not the only account of Life in Spirit, that are being told in the same terms by many other communicating Spirits received by serious, trustworthy and authentic mediums. Very few of these accounts have so far found their way into print in the English language. However, they abound in other languages, especially in Spanish and Portuguese, to say nothing of some notable books in French.

We believe this small book received through the hands of a dedicated medium by automatic writing to be authentic, having studied many other such writing received by many different mediums, totally unknown one to the other, at different times, in many different countries and languages.

We leave each reader to contemplate this information and to meditate upon the logic and rationality of these concepts. Remembering that all about us the Law of Cause and Effect is in action. Surely it is logical to conceive that we build today the life we shall lead tomorrow when we find ourselves beyond the veil, entering the next phase of existence.

Life is eternal! We are immortal! We had better believe it so we can start living constructively, thereby creating a better life and greater happiness for ourselves now, and in the future.

The editor

Part I

1
My Prayer

This book, "The Shadows Lifted from Death", has been given by one who claims to have Life after being certified in a perfectly lawful manner as "dead". The certificate of his death was granted by a responsible medical attendant, and thereafter his body was consigned to its burial place.

All these matters were carried out in a most respectable and orthodox way; yet this man, after having been dealt with so nicely, has left his physical body, and, encased in another covering more suitable to his changed environment - lives on.

To add to the impropriety of his conduct he actually travelled far in practically unknown spaces betwixt Heaven and Hell, to gain information of Life Continuous.

Unabashed by the certification of his death, this one is fully content to aver that he is more alive now than he was before!

To those who lack courage to face death with equanimity, or fail to have the strength of conviction that their loved ones are alive and enjoying life after being ceremoniously labelled "dead", this post mortem history is especially brought to their notice to give them courage and confidence.

What has occurred to one man, must necessarily occur to all men and women. God's laws are for all and not for individuals. Whether you believe or disbelieve what I have caused to be written here, is your responsibility, and as such it rests with you to lift the shadows, or - to be overcast by them.

The question is between your spirit and your blindness, and will surely be answered when the call from God reaches you.

My hope and fervent wish is that your blindness will be overcome, and that you will be able to see the so-called 'Angel of Death' as the deliverer and guide to a brighter and better continuation of Life.

That God's blessing may aid you in your decision is my prayer.

2
Background Remarks

There is every probability that the meaning of much that follows will be slightly obscure. Never mind - go on, for the text is not always the essence of the context. It is by stringing ideas in a rope or chain that enables the details to be placed in their proper sequence.

As a start we think that something should be known about those who are preparing the ideas and knowledge that will be embodied in this manuscript. There are four of us immediately concerned, but others are available and in reach if we need scientific or similar professional advice. We are "Dead" men speaking across the gulf that divides the two worlds. Not always were we so, for it seems only a short time ago that we were ourselves perplexing our minds and bodies over the self-same mundane matters that many of you are now doing.

I, myself was born in Lincolnshire of what I then considered to be very good parentage. My father indulged in intellectual pursuits, and my mother was of the 'World' - a sufficient satisfaction in itself to her. My father was only too pleased to recognise in me many of the traits that so distinguished his own outlook on life. From my mother I inherited a cynical view-point on all matters outside my immediate influence. I was considered to have been educated to a degree suitable to the condition in which I lived and had my being.

There were other members of the family, but for the purpose of these writings I am not going to introduce them. They have no concern with this at any time. It must not be inferred that I deprecate their presence or their mode of life; they are mentioned only to give clarity to this history.

I am not going to give a garrulous account of my life whilst in the physical body, and only sparse particulars to explain my mental and organic condition.

I was 32 years of age when, having acquainted myself with the habits and modes of the world of my day, I decided to travel to obtain further insight. Religion had only a small place in my thoughts. As the fact that one day I should have to leave my physical body was abhorrent to me I rapidly passed it to the back of my mind. I was quite unable to perceive that my destiny was not in my own hands, and felt myself quite competent to guide it.

In my travels I met many who tried to interest me in matters outside the dimensions I had established to suit my own convenience, but I spurned all their efforts to enlighten me. One man in particular I so treated - to my subsequent regret - who endeavoured to do his utmost to persuade me to perceive that there is more in life than that which I could see or grasp by my material senses. I have met that man since and realised how much sorrow and pain I should have saved myself had I but listened to him. But I must cease these self-scourging; there is no bitterness now.

During my visit to a foreign country, and while travelling through North Africa, I contracted one of the prevailing diseases, and after a period of illness and prostration, died. During the progress of my illness I had had no thought of dying, so it is not at all remarkable that the cessation of my physical activities gave me a profound shock as soon as I was in a condition to realise it.

The details of my life after bodily dissolution will be given in a more intimate manner with the hope that it may be of educational and spiritual value to those who are willing to learn.

3
My Arrival

It is not necessary to go into the varied details of my passing, of leaving the physical body to be enfolded in a spiritual one. For when the actual time for disassociating myself arrived I was in a very passive state; worn out and tired through the effort of endeavouring to cling to my body.

To an onlooker, had there been one, it must have appeared very painful. To me, all pain had left me; I was in that very pleasurable condition usually known as "floating".

I do not mean to say that I had not experienced pain, for I had, prior to the intimate knowledge given me that I was leaving the world. It had caused me great perturbation of mind when I first perceived that this was bound to be the result of my illness. I frantically made every endeavour to remember early teachings, and all I had heard regarding death and the hereafter. But all these thoughts became so incoherent that I was so bewildered and saddened by my attempts, that I lost the power to retain them in their proper sequence.

It was now that I thought with despair of the man who had so often endeavoured to enlighten me with the results of his own investigations into the future life, and the evidence he had deduced from facts he had obtained. But it was a hopeless struggle from the beginning. I had never seriously listened, so my mind had no recollection or remembrance. Soon I gave up the struggle, feeling that whatever it was it was now too late to affect the issue.

A deep feeling of lassitude pervaded the whole of my being, and I lay back, waiting for whatever might happen - final dissolution or - more life?

After a time, how long I know not, I noticed a man, a Doctor from his appearance, beside my bed. He smiled at me confidently and asked me if I was ready to move. There seemed to be something strange in his speech, but I was unable to trace the exact difference at the time. I frowned, thinking how ignorant he must be not to be aware that I was far too weak to move, and did not reply.

He stooped and placed his arms around me and I felt his comforting strength as he lifted me into a sitting position. In a very short time I found I could stand upright, then, that I was walking with comparative ease out of the room, my arm clasping that of the Doctor's.

I realised that I was listening to what he was saying, and yet he did not appear to be actually speaking. It was all very strange although I had no feeling of fear. I remember saying to myself I must ask him how he managed to restore me to health so quickly, just as he turned and asked if I felt fit enough to undertake a short journey. Upon my replying in the affirmative we then set out towards a destination whose goal was as yet unknown to me.

4
Reflections

It was now time for reflection for it appeared to me that matters had gone beyond my control. I must either be asleep and dreaming, or in so mentally an alert condition that I was actually visualising physical activity. That I was standing upright and walking beside my companion was very apparent to my mind. But was I really using my muscles for this purpose, or was it a dream, so vivid that it seemed real?

I glanced at my associate, but he seemed unaware of my deep uneasiness and proceeded to go forward slowly as if in silent contemplation of a subject that apparently caused him some slight amusement, judging by the faint smile that curved his lips and was reflected in his eyes.

Being reluctant to pose a question to him, so obvious that it might have invited an equally obvious reply that I was in full possession of all my senses and muscular action, I lapsed again into my own thoughts.

What really has happened? I pondered. Shall I soon find that I am still lying on my bed, feverish and with a wandering mind, or have I unknowingly done something that has taken me out of my body? This thought caused me to frown and give a puzzled sigh. I looked around me. Yes, I was on a road edged with grass on either side, an avenue. Light was flowing down from overhead, from the sun I imagined, although I was unable to see it owing to the thick foliage. There was a refreshing breeze blowing that invigorated me as I breathed it. That I was really breathing, and was also able to smell, was evident from the rise and fall of my chest and the keen appreciation of my nostrils to the perfume of the flowers.

This reflection caused me to ponder if any other matter-of-fact thing about myself was discernible. My hands and feet appeared to be unaltered, and on looking down at my clothes I saw I was wearing the rough but easy-fitting suit of darkish brown which I affected when going for a jaunt into the country or on a visit of investigation. While well-made, the clothes purposely did not betray any marked characteristic, so that neither my profession nor mode of life could be judged from them.

It was certainly my suit. But even as I decided this point a thought struck me in a very real and vivid manner. This particular suit had been left behind at my home, prior to my starting on my travels and so could not possibly be with me now! This caused a feeling of apprehension to steal over me again. I faltered and hesitated.

The "Doctor", who in noticing my agitation had quickly banished whatever thoughts had been occupying his mind, asked me at once what was causing the disturbance, and why I was fearful.

I studied him for a short time in silence, and he submitted to my scrutiny without any visible sign of embarrassment. He looked to be of middle age with a strongly marked face. Not handsome, I decided, at least not in the sense that some well-known and popular public figures are depicted as being handsome, but he had an inner earnestness that illuminated his features. His eyes were really the gateway to his deep understanding, for they now expressed concern at my evident conflict, yet gave a confidence that strengthened me.

Of his dress, or as much of it as showed under his coat, seemed to be of an every-day pattern, comfortable and well-used.

A gentleman and no prig, was my somewhat smug reflection.

5
Contemplation

To be explicit I must pause here to define my reactions. I now perceived that all my imaginings were only leading to one conclusion, and that I must at all costs seriously consider my position.

I was, to all appearances perfectly normal, without a trace of illness, but with a feeling of weakness as though I had lately been unaccustomed to walking. Yet in spite of this a tumult was going on within my mind. Was it caused by that dim suspicion I had so forcefully thrust into the background that I had passed out of life? Might that be the true reason for my emotions or were there other features that I had not taken into consideration?

I was never an easy man to deceive, and I had no desire to be duped at this stage of these strange proceedings. It might however, be more tactful for the moment to restrain my impulse and not to blurt out what I considered to be the essence of the truth in all the happenings I had so recently undergone.

I was seething with suspicion of this man who walked so tranquilly beside me. I had determined at the first meeting that he must be a Doctor, but now I was distinctly doubtful of my guess. The best course I could pursue, I concluded, would be to go on apparently unconcerned and seize the first opportunity that presented itself to escape from his company.

I formulated the desire to say to the man that I was now strong enough to go my own way unaccompanied, but something restrained me from doing so. I was unable to reason this out, so I said, "Where are we going? I feel too weak to walk very far."

"It is only just over the slight incline you see before you" he smiled. "There is my house in which I hope you will rest for a short time. You look as though you need rest and refreshment".

"A devilish nice fellow, on the surface", I thought, " so suave and pleasant, but I am not going to be duped by an accomplished rascal. At any rate he will not get much reward from robbing me".

"My travelling vouchers were not on my person and the small sum of money I carried would not be obtained without a struggle. The thought amused me. I laughed and said, "I am afraid I shall not be able to reimburse you for your hospitality as I have not the necessary money with me. But when I return to my home I will do so".

He looked at me attentively. "Yes, when you return home you will be able to do so", he replied gently.

We proceeded in silence until we reached the top of the slight incline, and then pausing, I saw a prettily built house that reminded me of the Chalets I had visited in Switzerland. To my view it seemed to be very solidly built, with sloping roofs and a veranda on the outside that went all round the building. The windows appeared to be surrounded by a curiously misty blue light that gave the house a very peaceful and restful aspect. There was a porch in front, and I perceived a studded door of a most becoming pattern. Well-kept gardens surrounded it, with familiar and unfamiliar flowers growing therein. Its aspect was very charming, and as the day was rather warm, the inviting look of the house had a very strong appeal.

It was apparent that my companion was able to sense my feelings. "Charmingly situated, isn't it? A place where rest should be obtained quite easily, you agree?"

I looked at him doubtfully. This was the second time he had shown that he knew of what I had been thinking without having heard any spoken words from me; the first lime being when I had begun to doubt his integrity and the possibility of his attempting to rob me. All very confusing and discomforting to one in the sort of predicament in which I was placed. In a strange land, alone, recovering from a serious illness, how should I be able to resist? Should this man have accomplices it would be much worse. Certainly the only thing for me to do was to carry out my plan to appear gullible and unsuspecting. I hurried forward towards the entrance at the front of the house being anxious to examine the terrain and ascertain what my future prospects of escape might be.

6
Unexpected Revelations

On entering the house we proceeded along a short passage to where a door gave entrance to a room lighted by some artificial means, the source of which was not apparent. My companion motioned me to seat myself in one of the padded chairs scattered about, which looked as if they were only waiting to give someone rest and comfort.

By this time I was only too pleased to lower myself into one, and relax. My companion pulled another chair near to mine and seated himself. He then said, smilingly, "I imagine it is time for me to introduce myself and perhaps allay some of the suspicions in your mind?"

I sat forward, a little startled. Here was the same thing occurring again, a species of mind-reading, realistically correct.

"It would prevent misunderstanding if we both introduced ourselves", I replied rather huskily.

"Shall I begin?" said this alarming personage.

"I had news of your arrival from a source with which you are unacquainted, so I went to the outskirts of our territory and awaited your approach. You must know that we can reach you, but may not infringe on your conditions except under circumstances of a particular nature. It would be better, perhaps, it I mentioned that I have known you for a long period; in fact I have sometimes been nearer to you than many of your companions".

The hearing of this extraordinary statement made me stare. I was quite unable to determine if I was listening to a sane man or to one mentally unbalanced. I was convinced however that it was very necessary to listen, so said, "Please continue. I will follow your words without interruption, I promise".

He went on - "You have been unaware of my surveillance and interest, but I can assure you that what I have told you really took place".

"When you were taken ill and your illness became so increasingly grave that it was necessary for you to leave the world you then inhabited and to pass on to another, I was informed of your passing. I watched you leave your bed of sickness, assisted by others of our State, although you failed to see them, and I have been with you until now".

He paused, and then added impressively, "Cast out of your mind the idea that I am not sound in my reasoning faculties, for I can assert with every degree of confidence that if "reasoning" could be measured, you would find my mind at this moment clearer than your own. You see I left your world many years previous to your own leaving it, so I am less bewildered. You are not dead as you can easily perceive by looking around, seeing trees, sky, houses; so what really has happened to both of us? In reality we simply passed from one space or time of life into another that is as real as the one we have left.

"You no doubt notice that I speak in the plural, for what happened to me has likewise had the same effect on you. You are "dead" to the world you knew, but are alive with an intensity of which you are unaware at present, in this one. I hope my explanation is clear, if not you can ask me at your leisure about any points you are at a loss to understand".

After this long explanation he sat back and watched me with smiling eyes as if he, himself, were acquainted with my difficulty in understanding his information.

To say that I was dumbfounded was a mild way of expressing my feelings, for I was bewildered and not a little frightened. Had I really died, in the sense that I had left one world and entered another? That I was in full preservation of my senses I did not doubt; the idea that it had been a dream had been cast out for some time now. So there was only one logical explanation if I was to believe my ears. Yet it did not seem possible.

The man who had given me all this information looked, and I am positive was, as solid as myself, perhaps more so, for I was unable to observe any traces of fatigue in him. I felt like a child who has lost its parents, and all around were unfamiliar sights. Under the circumstances I had to accept this strange assertion that I was dead, but moving, acting, and speaking like a person fully alive. A fantastic proposition, but certainly real!

I turned to my informant. You have either said too much or too little. That point I am unable to discover at this moment. I think it would be better for my sanity if you were to continue. First tell me who you are; where exactly I am: and what is the whole purpose of my being here with you".

He answered readily, "You must be prepared for a long story, so if there is anything you require to assist you in relaxing, so as to feel at ease while you are listening, ask for it before I begin".

I told him, to excuse my impatience, that I was so anxious to hear his tale that I felt I should obtain no relief until I had heard it, adding, "it seems so strange that all my previous ambitions appear to have evaporated before this gigantic puzzle with which I am confronted".

"Well", he began. "You must already have the knowledge that you have been ill, also as a result of that sickness - although of this you may still be unaware - you died. Your body still lies on the bed where you left it, being prepared for burial. This need cause you no shock, for you will not want that body again, so what better thing can be done than to return it to earth from which it was originally obtained? At least that part which constituted its main portion. The body you now have has been enveloped in the physical one, and is now released. You have always had your present one, but were unable to notice it owing to the thickness of the other which you have now cast off. It is as if you had left the outer portion behind, and now move and have your being in an inner one. This is the change that has taken place. A little drastic you may think, but really not very exciting. You are not concerned when you remove the coat which perhaps you were wearing out of doors, and then find yourself clad in one more suitable for the interior of the house, are you?"

He stopped and smiled. "That is how your transition appears to me; nothing more than you are now wearing or perhaps I should correctly say - using, a covering for your real self or soul, better suited to the conditions in which you are now. You will be in this state for a period commensurate with the needs of your soul's progression. An explanation of this I will leave to a later date, and will pause only to reassure you that you are alive and in full possession of all your faculties.

"Before I met you, there was a danger of your encountering those who would have taken advantage of your incapacity to go forward to places and persons with whom you were acquainted and who would have befriended you. Nay, there was a further and deeper danger that not only might you have been lost, but you might have been guided into most undesirable neighbourhoods, where you would have met those who would have preyed upon you; and then those fears of a financial loss you entertained earlier would have been realised".

His eyes twinkled as he noted my embarrassment. Once again he had proved his ability to read my unexpressed thoughts.

"Your life up to this stage", he went on, "has been very self-centred, and so those who might have helped you were prevented from doing so by your complete lack of interest. It was a grave failing, but fortunately greater danger was prevented through the help of those who have had charge of you during my peregrinations of the world of matter. They sent for me, told me of your plight and asked me to do service to you.

They selected me, knowing of my interest in you and of how I had tried on different occasions to get acquainted with you. I gladly complied with their wishes, not only because it had been requested of me, but also because they coincided with my own desire. I was anxious to meet you and give you the benefit of any knowledge I had gained during my sojourn here. It will be news to you to hear that I am a relative of yours; you are in fact my own grandson. I, you have never seen; you, I have seen only imperfectly; but I am fully cognisant of all the things you have done. I know of the situations through which you have passed, and have either left in a more hopeless state than when you entered, or those cases that have benefited by your approach and knowledge of their peculiar difficulties"

I gazed beseechingly at my companion and begged him to cease. The whole matter now seemed to be of such monstrous growth that my mind was unable to contain it. Time in which to digest what he had told me was what I most urgently needed. The means to be able to focus the problem was beyond my grasp. I craved for rest and solitude.

My Grandparent - for if what he had told me was true, I had better accustom myself to it - noticed my agitation and nodded solemnly but in a whimsical way.

"Yes", he smiled, "I suppose all this is really a shock to your preconceived ideas. To be alive; to be greeted by a personage who allegedly died years before you were born, and who is yet talking to you, giving you advice and in full possession of his senses; cannot fail to be bewildering. It needs a big change in thought so that it can be reasonably assimilated. Take all the time you require; sleep, and upon your awakening we will dwell on those points that still elude you".

Sleep? That appeared to be the most unlikely thing I should be able to accomplish. My mind was revolving like a top; I was unable to contain my bewilderment and agonising surprise at all that had happened to me. How long had I been in this land of dreams - or stark reality?

I put that question to my host and received a reply to the effect that only one day and a night had passed according to earth-time. Yet what had been achieved in such a short period! I had died; found myself alive; had been recognised by one who had been, and still was, interested in my life; and had been made acquainted with matters that were still beyond my comprehension.

Whilst all these thoughts were flooding my mind, a feeling of lassitude began to pervade my being. It may have been caused by my late illness, or the calming gaze of my companion may perhaps have assisted it, for, suddenly, struggle against it as I would, I seemed to be stepping into a darkness that was slowly creeping towards me, blotting out the view from the windows and seeping into the interior of the room. It reached me, and a feeling of peace and serenity surrounded me. My thoughts became more restful. My last conscious feelings were of how good it would be to sleep now, and later wake up with the true explanation of my experiences. At that stage I must have become wholly unconscious for I had no remembrance of what immediately followed.

7
On Awakening

When I became aware that I was awake once more, it must have been a long time after the facts I have recorded. I now found that I was in a different room from the one in which I had fallen asleep. There was a restful, diffused light coming through the windows, and a particularly refreshing and invigorating breeze flowing through the room.

For a time I lay looking round this apartment. There seemed something reminiscent about it, but the exact association eluded me. It was an oblong room with casement windows all round. The divisions between the windows were so slight that at a distance it seemed to be entirely composed of sections of a pale tinted glass in small, thin frames. Looking upward I discerned that the ceiling was formed of similar coloured glass, if glass it was, and that there were small, shining shapes that gave light and lustre to the whole interior. I was fascinated as I gazed, for they seemed to me as though they were giving forth their brilliance entirely for my benefit. I was exceedingly puzzled as to the cause of their vivid attraction.

It was only after a long time that I could drag my eyes away from them very reluctantly, to glance round the rest of the room. There was a noticeable lack of interior ornamentation, but the windows gave a view of a rolling mass of greenery and flowers. Their very colours, impossible as it seemed, appeared to be reaching forth to give tribute of their own all powerful, stimulating life.

The herbage was in a way similar to that of the world, but there the similarity ended. Here were no bare and unsightly patches or downtrodden places. The grass was short, strongly woven together and seemed to invite me to go out and walk or ride down its comforting slopes. It appeared to have Life in a sense that I have never seen before. The flowers, as far as I could see were larger and finer than any I had previously known. Some were familiar, while others looked like rare types. There was a riot of colour, yet the right note had been struck in their unusual blending.

The perfume that pervaded my room was beyond description. No cloying or sickly scent, but a refreshing one that invited continuous appreciation.

My eyes now studied the room itself and its furnishings. I noticed that I was lying on a couch or divan that was most excellently sprung. I could feel its resilience as I turned, so that I seemed to be supported on all sides of my body as I reclined there. Its foot was composed of a material that glistened against a dark background, and some pattern was picked out in many colours which were in the material itself and not a later insertion.

A second couch to mine, but further away, and two comfortable armchairs were in the room. As I was concluding my survey I suddenly noticed a writing-desk or bureau with a chair drawn up conveniently near it. Speedy recollection then returned to me. With a few noticeable alterations this room was almost a replica of the room of which I had been so fond in my own home. The home that I had left forever when I had started out on my travels.

8
Further Information

Upon arriving at this conclusion, reaction set in and my thoughts were full of what my strange companion had told me prior to my sleep. There must be something in what he had said after all. Suppose I was dead - in the sense in which that word is usually known - yet more alive than I had ever been, even at my healthiest! How had I arrived in my present room? Who had prepared it for me? From whence had they obtained my favourite furniture? A host of questions formed themselves in my mind. Then a doubt swept over me once more. Were these things really solid or only the figment of my imagination? The couch on which I lay was certainly solid enough, I could feel its substantial strength under me.

At this thought I leaped up and placed my hands firmly on the chairs, following this by trying to rock the bureau. They were all as solidly substantial as it is possible for such articles to be, and appeared to have been cleaned and polished quite recently.

There was no trace of dust on any of them and the floor, which lacked carpet or rugs, was in a like condition.

The chance of further discoveries was denied me owing to the sound of steps outside and a knock at the door. I opened it to see a young man standing there apparently waiting my invitation to enter. This was a delightful surprise to me for it gave me the opportunity of obtaining answers to some of my questions. I at once requested him to enter and subjected him to a close scrutiny as he accepted my invitation.

He appeared to be a few years younger than I, with a very happy disposition, if his smiling face was any guide. The way he walked and his manner, assured me that he was in excellent health and very satisfied with his life.

Upon reaching one of the chairs, I indicated he should seat himself, and I took one of the others. The light was shining fully on his features and I could easily watch the trend of his thoughts on his mobile face.

He turned to me and said, "You must excuse the early visit I am paying you, but I was unable to resist the urge to be one of the first to congratulate you upon your arrival, and I hope this will be but the first of many more visits".

So they 'congratulate' you on dying, instead of grieving over it in this new world, I thought.

I assured my companion of the pleasure his visit gave me, adding, "Perhaps you would be good enough to answer some of the many questions I wish to ask?"

He laughed merrily as he answered, "I shall not be able to answer them all, but as your first one will certainly be to know if you are alive, I can earnestly assure you that you are; also that dreams, hobgoblins, or fantasy has not entered into any of the acts you have already encountered, nor do they at any time".

He then appeared to be convulsed with mirth and cried between bursts of laughter. "Isn't that - the doubt of your being alive - that is the predominant thought in your mind at the moment? Well, let me hit or pinch you, and then you will have physical proof, if you so desire. But without your consent I shall not proceed with this experiment, for you look wild enough to retaliate on me, if I did cause you some slight hurt".

At this sally I had to join in his laughter, and soon, due to his infectious gaiety, we were on a very friendly footing so that I felt I could safely ask even intimate questions without giving offence. I started to marshal the facts I most urgently required elucidating, and after getting them as nearly sorted as I was capable of doing, began my questionnaire.

"To commence with" I said, "please remember I am practically unaware of where I am or who I am. Am I myself or somebody causing me to masquerade as a traveller in an unknown country? My head is filled with conflicting ideas and I really wish to establish my exact status. Am I really the same person as I was previous to my supposed death, and am I now alive? Is it all lies we are taught that we have to wait for "The Resurrection"? Is there any truth in the teachings of the Church that Paradise is for the few, and eternal damnation for those of a different creed?"

"I had some faint belief that there really was another life, but neglected to give the question any study. It may have been folly not to have done so, and I am now going to try and make amends by earnestly seeking for the truth and following it wherever it may lead".

I gave all this in a burst of eloquence that surprised even me; and when I ceased, a feeling of relief overcame me, confirming my thought that the only way out of the maze of incoherent speculations was to enquire from someone who was in a position to enlighten me, and claim their help. Hence my anxiety to put forward my point of view regarding my transition.

My companion, who had regained his gravity during the early part of my outburst, had followed my words with extreme earnestness until I had finished. He then stood up and coming nearer to me said, "I am not in a position to answer all your questions, although I have been appointed to assist you in every conceivable way. Many of the questions you ask will be answered by yourself at a later period. Of that I am very certain".

"I can undoubtedly relieve your feelings by saying that you are really alive, and are not suffering from any mental derangement. Your time of arrival in this world - which is the one nearest to the material one you have so recently left - was known to us. Also arrangements were then made for you to be educated in the ways and meaning of our side of life. Do not hastily assume that there is a Judgement Seat waiting for your appearance, so that a verdict can be pronounced upon your past life, either good or bad; such a course of procedure is unknown here. There are certainly those who will wait upon you at a convenient period, who will go over with you the antecedent history of your life, and assist you in acknowledging the merits or demerits of all that was done. They will enquire as to what use you put the time in the material world that the Great Spirit allowed you, for the purpose of establishing the strength of character and love that is so necessary, if you are to have a worthy position here".

"I know that you had wealth, but that is now of so little value that you would be unable to give it away even if you had it with you. As to hate, jealousy, malice or selfishness, it would have been better if you could have left them buried under your wealth, hidden in an inaccessible place that, pray God, may never be found by those whom you have now left. But if you have brought with you toleration, understanding and love, then you can deem yourself wealthy indeed, for that is our coinage, and the one registering the greatest value, is "Love for All".

My companion paused as if to re-assemble his thoughts, then continued, "I think it will be more to your advantage in understanding these things, if you will accompany me on an exploration of the continent on which you now are, so that you can examine your surroundings, for I must inform you that this is not yet your permanent abiding place. That place has been determined upon by your own course of living, and by nobody else. You are now really a 'personage'; for any cloak of pretence you may have previously put on to cover up your own thoughts or to deceive others, has gone for ever. You will be seen astrally, by all and sundry, as you have made yourself, so think not that you will be able to confuse others as to your real Self. Frankly, deceit is impossible here and it is well that it operates in that way, for only those suited to this environment can live here in any degree of comfort. This is the working of a perfect law; a law which is unknown to men".

"So now let us sally forth and see how it works".

9
My New Abode

In company with my new friend I fared forth, hoping that by actually seeing things for myself I might be able to clear the fog from my mind. What I was going to see or learn was still beyond my comprehension, but I was determined to give all a fair hearing and withhold judgement until I had further facts, from which to make deductions.

If what I had already heard was any criterion of what God had prepared for me, then I was anticipating a revelation that - if I had the power to do so - would shake the foundations of the world I had left, out of all its beliefs and theories.

My companion must have caught the trend of my thoughts for he turned and said, "Yes, God's providence towards His children is something beyond all worldly knowledge. It is indeed beyond the knowledge of the Heaven in which you are now. We perhaps, can see and know a little more than you can at present; but beyond our perception is something so vast that when we contemplate it we are forced to draw a cloak over our minds, so as to prevent our becoming dazed and bemused, so unable are we to comprehend such glories,

"How many aeons of time may pass before we shall be able to live in such perfection, I am unable to give any idea. But we really know that when we are ready we shall go forward, imbued with the knowledge and having the power to frequent the place that has been prepared for us".

As my friend spoke I sensed an underlying ardency, that seemed to speak to me wistfully of the yearning he was experiencing to go in search of the excellence he only dimly saw.

Throwing aside his earnestness, he laughed. "It would be well if I introduced myself to you now I think. My name was once Ralph Littlewood, gentleman. But now, Ralph the gatherer of those who, having lost one part of their life, are seeking something to replace it.

"My work, though treasured - for it is indeed the greatest of pleasure - is to assist those who foregather on our shores like the survivors of a shipwreck, not knowing when they landed or where they are going. Some looking forward to a better land, others indifferent; and a few with a knowledge of the geography of the place they are in. The latter, alas are few in number; the other categories being much greater!

"You, my friend are in the middle condition nearly approaching the first, so I must of necessity guide your footsteps so that you can advance and quench the thirst that is now consuming you to go forward and prospect this new hemisphere in which you find yourself.

"The first warning I must now give you, is to realise that for a time everything may appear normal, but out of alignment with your views. You are in a condition not far removed from that of your Earth, so you will find some characteristics and oddities to which you are accustomed. But when you examine these more closely you will receive a surprise, for they will not answer to the usual tests you apply; they will prove to be different. Let me give you an example of what I mean.

"A man usually passes through life eating, drinking and sleeping and, on some rare occasions, meditating on matters outside of his physical senses. From these he derives material and physical comfort, and a brightening of his intellect; but he is never really satisfied that all he desires has been attained; there is always something of his aspirations left unassuaged. Yet, when he arrives on our plane of existence, he finds that he has the same desires and endeavours to supply their wants as hitherto.

"He then discovers that his physical and material side is very easily satisfied, by being unsatisfied with what he gives them. The reason being that this source of supply is not needed, and when he fully realises this, he leaves them and the appetite for such sustenance is lost. But, paradoxically, the need for thoughtful meditation increases in proportion to the time and intellectual provender that is used. Thus the needs of the mind increase in ratio, as those of the physical and material decrease.

"This is a very essential difference when it is calmly and dispassionately reviewed. A wise apportionment of food and sleep are not of great merit with us, but those who keep their minds vividly and fully conscious receive their own reward by having a keener urge to attain their most laudable expression. This may not be very clear to you on your first discernment, but it will reach you with a greater force at a later period".

As we were speaking, I noticed that we were approaching what I imagined to be some small town or city. I pointed this out to Ralph, saying that I was rather surprised that such a grouping of houses and people were necessary.

He retorted, smilingly. "Are you surprised? Do not people always desire to herd together in your world, and so have their habitations converging for this express purpose? Why then should you imagine that they should at once change the habits of their minds? Some I know prefer solitude, but on investigation it will be found that there are those who, either openly or secretly, have contained within themselves this particular wish and so are granted its fulfilment as soon as it is possible to do so.

"There is an alteration in your body once you have passed through the Great Change, but not of your mind. That has to be disciplined and fed in the usual manner by experience and association with those ideas that give permanent growth. The Mind, and all that that word portends, is practically unknown in the world you have left, but it is the one thing that is unaffected by so-called Death.

"If you will closely examine those you are going to meet, I am perfectly sure this fact will be obvious to you, even at this early stage of your visit".

I looked forward eagerly to see if there was anything different in the appearance of this town from that to which I was normally accustomed, but with the exception that there was a total absence of any smoke being emitted from the chimneys, I could see nothing unusual. The houses certainly appeared to be slightly more spacious than customary, but they had the same shapes, ornamentations, and designs as those I had known. People were moving about in a manner with which I was well acquainted and gave no occasion for surprise.

10
An Interesting Experience

The approach to this town seemed to be so real that I began again to feel unreal myself. Why should it be, I asked mentally, that one part of my mind was recognising familiar surroundings, while another part of that same mind was endeavouring laboriously to familiarise itself with new ideas and environments?

Involuntarily I looked at Ralph to see if he appreciated the complexity of the whole thing as it applied to me, but he seemed to be deep in some inner complexity of thought that was causing him to crease his brow and frown slightly.

I glanced away from him again on seeing this, and then perceived two persons approaching us. They were men engaged in conversation that appeared to be of deep interest to them. They were dressed in some kind of nondescript clothing that did not betray anything that might give an indication as to their mode of life. They walked and talked together as I had seen many others do, prior to my passing to this place. It was with some natural eagerness that I awaited their progress, for I could see that if they continued on their present course, we should meet. Ralph looked up. His eyes twinkled as he saw the men, and turning to me he said "Now you will have an opportunity to test ideas you may have formed recently. These two will endeavour to give you guidance and illuminating counsel. It will be given with the greatest assurance and authority. It will sound a little remote, perhaps, but they will produce it to support their contentions. Do not hesitate to speak with them for they will delight in your conversation".

Then seeing that the men were within reach of his voice he cried, "Well, friends, what is this matter that engrosses you so much that you are unable to notice our approach?"

The men momentarily halted, looked round, and one called out, "It is you then, Ralph". Then seeing me he continued. "And who is the stranger with you? At least he appears so to us, but of course he may have come from another part of this world. This realm of latent consciousness, created by a desire to escape from worldly realities".

His friend hearing this, turned and objected. "Nay, George, your tongue runs before your wit. It is a land of desire created to satisfy senses and emotions; caused by mass thought by those whose sole ambition it is to escape from physical sensation and be among those of aesthetic taste".

Then, seeing my dumbfounded look at hearing these unimaginable assertions, he continued. "Also you, young man! Do not listen to the false impressions and views that your friend " - pointing to Ralph - "will give you. I grant that he is a plausible and very convincing person, but beware of lying teachers and prophets. Has it not been written and said on innumerable occasions that the glamour of a well used tongue will cloud the mind of the most earnest seeker after truth?"

As he ceased, they both turned and looked at us expectantly, especially at me, giving a fair resemblance of some athlete eager to start his race.

My confusion so overcame me that I refrained, through sensitiveness, to look toward Ralph. It was soon apparent, however, that he was entirely unperturbed at this assault, for he cried gaily. "Go on! You have my leave to convince the stranger with us that all I have told him is untrue".

Upon my considering this view for a moment, there appeared to be only one thing that might fit this category, and that was the fact that he had stated or inferred, that I had died in one place and was now living in another. Should I therefore have to rely in future on information from other sources as to how I had actually arrived?

Noticing that there was an expectant pause and that all of them were looking towards me, awaiting my reaction to their words, I remarked, "What you have stated can be interpreted in various ways, all of which, if taken separately may have a modicum of truth, but if massed together proclaim a glaring inconsistency with the whole of the facts. It is true that I am entirely unaware of my manner of entrance to this world. But I do know that something beyond my power to comprehend at present has caused this upheaval in my life. I had always attributed this transition as being the work of God, but how it has all been accomplished I must leave to discover until I have gained more knowledge.

"It is very apparent to me that you two men are in the same turmoil of mind. Ralph must be an exception, for, from his unconcerned air he either knows more of this mystery, or is supremely indifferent to this aspect of which we are so puzzled. I am trying to be as impartial as is possible for one with an emotional sense that is liable to distrust cold logic".

Upon hearing this Ralph smiled. With slightly twitching lips he replied. "So you are not convinced that you are the creation of a mind or an emotion? If you had been I should have asked you to consider who or what, produced either of these creators. There must have been a beginning, however far away it might seem, and a particular sense, however strong it may be, surely started from **something**! What say you, friends?"

The two men hastened to answer him in concert, and then turned a torrent of words on each other. I was quite unable to glean any sense from their rapid exchanges, so I looked appealingly at Ralph and turned away.

He at once approached me and throwing an arm round my shoulder said. "These gentlemen disputed all things during their material life, and the habit has persisted. You must know that there is no coercion here. It is not allowed, for Justice cannot permit interference. What you are, is what you have made yourselves, and only upon your own realisation that some alteration is necessary, can things be changed. But again, you must change it. No other person can do it for you. If that were possible so many here would be living lives other than their own. The wisest among us cannot obtrude, but they may give advice from their garnered wisdom. They will willingly do so to any who frankly ask for such advice.

"This is the reason why I have not, up to this time, endeavoured to influence you. This attitude will be changed anon, for I see the awakening of a glimmering of leaven in your mind. This is all to the good, for, until the mind is ready, new ideas or new avenues of approach are not received in a friendly spirit. Much that will appear to be contradictory will be presented to your view and you must endeavour to gain all you can from what is shown you.

"Shall I begin? Well then, those two men we have just left have exhibited to you what was their main interest in earthly life - to catalogue everything under a definite name. They cannot realise that certain joys or sorrows cannot be so classified.

"For instance, can you ever enter in some supposed category the music in the song of a bird? Can you put into words the throbbing of ecstasy in its love note, or the quivering of its small body as its wings endeavour to keep in tune with its voice? You know that this is beyond the power of the most eminent of those who create music or poetry. It is only something within yourself that recognises all that loveliness; but it remains, and will remain, unclassifiable. It is the God-like power within that bird that echoes within you and joins with a similar radiation that is thrusting itself forward to join that from which all beauty comes".

11
Confronting an Unexpected Reality

Ralph ceased speaking, but for some time after he had done so I was striving to restrain my eagerness to implore him to continue. Evidently sensing my impatience to hear more, he added.

"You must bear in mind that you are still in a World that is very near to the one you have so recently left. So the appearance and the buildings of this town are very similar to those to which you have been accustomed. It would be bad policy to allow new visitors here to be startled by what they see, as usually they arrive bewildered and uncertain of themselves. Anything that would add to that bewilderment might produce such confusion that long periods would have to elapse before this chaotic condition would be eradicated, so of course the outward surroundings are made to look familiar.

"You, yourself have noticed this, but yet you expected something quite different, didn't you?" He asked with a quizzical smile. "There are, of course differences, as you will soon see, and it will give me great pleasure to show them to you. Come, follow me then, and you will be able to satisfy your eagerness to learn the why's and the wherefore's of this strange Planet".

He then hurried me forward towards a large building in a street of the town. From its appearance I should judge it was used for meetings and similar gatherings. As we approached I noticed a great number of people were all converging towards it. I glanced interestedly at the faces of those nearest me. In some I saw hope and expectancy, whilst in others downright despair.

Feeling perplexed about this, I asked Ralph the meaning of this despairing condition, as, if these persons have survived death I failed to understand their misery. They should, I thought, have had happy expressions, for the greatest bugbear of their earthly existence had been lifted from them.

Casting my mind back I could very easily pick up the feeling that I, and others generally, had experienced when we had had to approach the bodies of those whom we wrongfully described as being 'dead'. The answer to the eternal question we had so often formulated- 'Where are they now? - was at this moment, and to my own mind, completely and happily answered. Why then the foreboding expressions on the faces of these people, I asked myself.

Ralph, with his uncanny intuition - or was it pre-knowledge - answered all this without the need of any vocal questions from me.

"It is quite common knowledge that the majority of mankind have been taught that there is a dreadful Judgement Day before them, when an account must be given of all your work whilst in a physical body. All these people you see are comparatively new arrivals; although on the outskirts, watching and waiting, are those who have been here for longer periods.

We will leave those for awhile and confine our attention to those who are newcomers.

"They have been told by others that they must gather in this building to hear from one who is well able to inform them, when and how they should conduct themselves; also what is the result of their sojourn in the late world of existence. To many this will indeed be the Judgement Day, although in a totally different sense than the one generally associated with it.

"Let us enter and listen, for your own life will also be portrayed for accountancy and investigation. Do not be nervous, remember I shall stay by your side, and if there are any points that I consider need elucidation, I will explain them".

I felt very sure here, that if anybody had passed a comment on my facial appearance at that moment of hearing this information, they would easily have recognised a puzzled and rather apprehensive look. For now I was filled with terrors and foreboding.

All those things which formerly I had ashamedly kept in the background of my mind, came forward and appeared to exhibit grotesque shapes and powers.

As I pondered, these fears grew stronger and more formidable until they filled me with a great horror. I knew I had committed a number of things that I had never contemplated would become known. Now all these were to be brought out publicly, and I should be unable to stem the flow of the recital of all those miserable acts I had created by my own selfishness and lack of restraint.

What to do now, I was unable to think. I was held there by my own misgivings as to the ultimate result. It was useless to think of flight. Where was I to go if I did, and where could I hide? I was enmeshed in a tangled web and had no strength to break out. If before doing these things I had really thought that they would ever become known, were there any that I should not have been guilty of committing? Well, it was useless to quibble at what was now going to happen. I must make payment for them in whatever token would be required of me.

Upon reaching this decision, I joined the throng of those passing into the Hall, not caring if Ralph followed or not; inwardly hoping that he would desert me. For although I had only known him for such a short space of time, I should be glad if he did not listen to the recital of my life-history.

12
The Meeting Hall

Upon reaching the interior of the Hall, I found it was arranged in galleries so that everyone was able to see the whole room clearly. At the back was a tastefully arranged dais, a little higher than the main floor of the building. There were windows all round, that by some strange facet of architecture allowed the light to reach the dais and then diffuse itself into the Hall.

I was unable to see anybody seated on this platform, but noticed that there was a door at the rear which I presumed gave entrance to those who were to address the meeting. With great interest I now turned towards the occupants of the galleries and saw that gangways leading to all parts were being kept clear by attendants. By this time the seats were nearly all occupied by men and women and, to my surprise, by children of all ages. The latter were apparently in charge of an adult, and were laughing excitedly.

The whole effect was exactly as if an audience was awaiting the appearance of some popular figure, but with this notable difference - the majority were plainly apprehensive of **what** they were to see. A murmur of voices broke out: some of the men were gesturing towards the front of the Hall as if to emphasise their words. I stood there, undecided and troubled, until I felt a tap on my shoulder, and turning sharply saw it was Ralph who had touched me.

"Do not let fear enter into your being", he warned. "It is the greatest curse that you can harbour. It destroys your strength, weakens your intellect, and allows hate and envy to enter. Your soul - your whole being - will be crushed and warped beyond all control should fear predominate. Thrust it forth and go your way undisturbed by the fancies and fables of your youth and childhood. God is not mocked and he is not a revengeful God. That which you will see and hear is not the judgement of a diabolical mind, but of Justice. You will be given an understanding of yourself such as has never been presented to you before, and all will be well.

"You will be unable to shake me off until my purpose is accomplished, which is to give you enlightenment at this momentous crisis of your existence. Let us go and sit down in those two seats in the centre which are unoccupied".

Unable to answer, I followed him dumbly to the seats he had indicated, and we sat down.

I noticed that the attendants had stood respectfully aside as Ralph preceded me, and after we had comfortably seated ourselves mentioned this fact to him. His reply was rather enigmatic, for he only stated that they had recognised him by his colour and so allowed him easy access. These seats, he added, had been reserved for our use; the attendants admitting his right, had freely allowed us to occupy them.

This was a complete mystery to me, so for the time I left it and turned my attention to my neighbours. The nearest was a man who seemed to be very aged, and scarcely to have recovered from a severe illness. Seated next to him was a young girl, who from all appearance was in perfect health. She was speaking to the old man and was apparently giving him words of cheer and encouragement, for I saw his lined and careworn face light up as she spoke. Their relationship was very patent. By the way they looked at each other it could only have been a daughter giving loving greetings to a fond parent after an absence of many years. Thus, anyhow, was the pattern as I formed it in my mind.

Suddenly I heard a bell with a very silvery and vibrant note sound out. The murmuring of the crowd ceased, and all eyes were turned anxiously toward the door at the back of the dais that I had previously noticed.

13
Initial Enlightenment

The door opened. A man entered and came forward to the centre of the dais. Although he was accompanied by two companions who took positions one on either side of him, it was clearly apparent that it was the first entrant who was the principal personage.

I gazed at this man with a great deal of interest, and no little trepidation. He appeared to be about thirty-five years of age, of medium height and moderate proportions, but his whole being radiated good health and affability. I seemed to discern, from the expression of his face, that he took a keen interest in his audience who were now all gazing upward watching him. As he noticed this his dark eyes glinted humorously, and a slight smile twitched his lips as he turned and spoke to the companion on his left.

The whole appearance of this Leader impressed me in a remarkable way. I felt that here was one who had passed through the whole gamut of human joys and sufferings, and had yet risen superior to all trials. In fact he appeared to have gained great strength and confidence from his experiences. Not that there was anything dominating about him, but impressiveness, evidently gained through knowledge, pervaded the whole of his being. Whoever had authorised him to take charge of these proceedings had made a discerning and very apt selection, was my unexpressed thought.

Turning again towards Ralph, I saw that he was evidently acquainted with the "Chairman", if I can so call him, for I had caught an answering smile directed to my companion, who must have undoubtedly greeted him in some way. Also I now noticed that between the two men there were marked similarities in their look and demeanour. I felt a quick certainty in my mind that these two were far more than passing acquaintances, they were old friends.

At this moment the Leader stepped forward a few paces in front of his colleagues, and, raising his hand for silence, waited for the subsidence of voices and movement. In a few minutes this was obtained, and an expectant silence hung over the Hall, as the people breathlessly awaited his words.

"My friends" he began in a clear voice, "you have all gathered here to obtain some knowledge of your present life and future homes. The latter are so far ready for your habitation in the sense that all that you have sent here in the shape of material has been made of use. But about this I will refer more directly, later in my speech.

"Firstly, I wish you to rid your minds of any idea that this is your Judgement Day, in the way in which you have been taught to understand that word. Instead it is a time of inner discernment, and that is all. Here is no picturesque Heaven, nor is there a Hell as imagined by those with minds that deem perpetual torture is incense to God. We here have neither of those places, but we certainly have a place for each one of you according to your deserts.

"By passing through a material world and possessing a physical body, you people have been preparing your spiritual body for its future environment. The spiritual covering is what you now have; your physical body has been left for ever, but during the time it was in use you formed your own minds and your characters. Those formed characteristics now inhabit your present bodies, and it is from their records that full justice will be done. Thus then, you see, there is no need for any Judge, for your own inner selves will pronounce the verdict on yourselves".

Here he paused, and looked out over the crowded sea of faces below him. Following his gaze, I saw the facial expressions of most of those present light up. I also felt my own spirit grow brighter. Doubtless my face also, was expressive of my enlightenment, for I heard Ralph give vent to a low chuckle, and he bent forward to hear what further the Speaker was going to add. I also turned eagerly toward the dais as the man continued his speech.

"The responsibility for whatever use you have made of your worldly life is entirely yours, not God's. He gave you Life and the ability to be able to understand what was right, and what would be injurious to the Spirit. He added to that the years you spent on the Earth, so that you could acquire experience and wisdom. To assist you on your journey, God has sent, throughout the ages, Teachers with knowledge of what He required of you, to teach you His simple laws. This has been done on numerous occasions, so that no person, whatever his colour or nationality, has been left in the dark as to the real meaning of an Earth-sojourn as a preparatory school for the life Eternal.

"There are those, who because of their primitive life have not been able to benefit in the manner of civilised peoples, yet they have received the same teaching through their near approach to the spirit of the woods, trees and of Nature, so all have been catered for in accordance with their respective needs. God being the Great Spirit of us all, desires you all to arrive before Him in due course. He recognises that you are all part of His creation and are, in reality, His children. No, this is not a figment of my imagination", he comforted his hearers, "but the teaching of those who have advanced a long way towards the Great Spirit. These are but passing down to you His wishes. Therefore the way is before you on which you shall travel. Prior to any advancement, however, a survey must be made as to your preparedness to undertake this journey".

A slight pause now ensued, as if to give time for the meaning of the words to sink fully into the minds of the listeners. Then raising his voice slightly, the speaker continued:

"As I previously stated, your homes are already built, but only as far as the building materials you have sent here allow. It is your thoughts and actions that have supplied that material, and so that you may understand the nature of that which you have prepared, the whole of your life-histories will be shown individually to each person present. Do not be apprehensive. Your neighbours will be unable to see your histories, neither can you see theirs, except only by consent of those that have the knowledge and wisdom to allow it.

"Here then is no question of the predetermination of your future state. That has all been arranged in accordance with your moral worth. Riches, fame or adulation is of no practical value, only sincerity counts. To be thus worthy you must have given and received Love. By this I do not mean love in an emotional sense, but that which has grown within you until it is your whole being, and in a real sense your life. Therefore those who have this gift are the possessors of far greater riches or fame than all the heaped-up jewels of the far-famed Indies, or the plaudits of the people given to a particular public favourite.

"God is all love and purity, so those who are worthy of His particular design must also travel His way and rest in those places He has caused to be provided for His travellers.

"This is a truth indeed that has unfortunately been overlooked so often that it has not been deemed necessary for many of you to seek it. Some of you have arrived here with set views as to their future, and how they are to live their new extension of life. They must have had some faint idea of the true facts as they are known here, although perhaps they were only dimly aware of it in their late world. Learn this. Your freedom of will is unimpaired and cannot be taken away from you. It is the forerunner of all spiritual worth, for without that freedom of choice you would never have made any effort. It can be used for progression or - for retrogression. That is the choice you yourselves will have to make.

"There is no one here who will be allowed to carry on their shoulders the sorrows of another, nor have the benefit of joys those others have earned. Therefore be warned by this. If any of you have fixed ideas that have great strength, examine them carefully before you make any move. Some have brought with them the preconceived notion that they will reside in some special place that has been jealously kept for them; looking on it as a prior right that they shall have this coveted seat or place. Well, they will certainly attain what they so greedily desire, for the mind has created that special niche for them. Yet those so inclined must remember that they will sit in this solitary splendour for aeons of time if so they wish, unmolested, still awaiting for that condition to materialise which they have previously visualised during their earth-life as being there. It will not be until the foolishness of those aspirations is fully realised, and understood by them, that they will descend from their friendless eminence to mix again with those they had previously despised and shunned, and give forth to their fellows the love that should rightly be shared by all.

"Here we have no favoured few. All are the same and worthy of the same consideration. So be tolerant, understanding, and the road to progress is open to you wherever you may be placed. The heights or the depths are yours in accordance with your will, and no other person can be considered to blame for whatever you, yourself, have done. Each one is worthy of his prize and so your compensation will be in agreement with the labour of love you have given to others".

14
My First Instructions

The Speaker ceased. A hush fell over the crowded hall; all faces were lifted to his. Then raising his arms over the assembly as though to invoke a blessing, he continued in a slow, steady voice. "I now ask that power be given unto all here, that they may understand and make use of this knowledge I have taught; each for their separate needs in compliance with the will of God and His great love".

As he finished his prayer, it appeared to me as if the roof of the hall had opened. A stream of coloured light poured down from above and bathed us all in its glow. I fell a tingling sensation pervade the whole of my being as if I had been inwardly illuminated by a radiation that was growing outwards.

My first feelings were of astonishment and strength, but as these subsided I became aware of a vividness of the mind that I had never previously experienced. I glanced toward the dais and saw that it was now unoccupied; the three men had left unobserved by me.

I looked round the hall: it was emptying fast; the people passing out by the various exits. Their faces looked vacant, stunned, as though puzzled by what they had heard. They were now being forced to search for something that had previously eluded them, which now for the first time presented itself for inspection and understanding.

Ralph who had remained silent beside me during the whole of the oration, now turned to me. I saw that he too was looking very serious. Without speaking he searched my face narrowly in a calm, reflective manner, then said steadily.

"You have learnt how Judgement is carried out from one who is fully competent to know the real meaning of all he says. He is a man who has passed through many things that are beyond your understanding at present but, owing to his wisdom and experience, he has been sent to give verbal guidance to all of those who were present in this hall, and who were waiting for instruction. You are one who will surely follow the teachings he has given; therefore, before the time of preparation let us openly speak of those things that are nearest the heart, but furthest from the mind.

"To encourage your confidence let me assure you that what you are to undergo is not a mythical experience or an hallucination, but only a reasonable occurrence if you will but cast your mind backward to your short earthly life. Did you dream that all those things that you have done, either good or bad, joyous or sorrowful, harsh or kind, were all obliterated by your transition? If so, you must have been very credulous, or you deluded yourself to a degree beyond normal comprehension.

"You, and all mankind, are put into earth life and exhorted to use physical existence for a definite purpose. Now the time has come to see what result has been achieved, and remember that there is no escape from his self-revealing examination.

"We who have been here longer have all had to make the

same search into our past lives, as a matter of course. Even now we occasionally have portions of that life portrayed to us, so that we may still benefit from its study. I have told you this because we are now going to the room where this examination can be made".

15
My Next Step

As we reached the open again, I glanced around to observe if there were any differences in the surroundings since my last appearance - how long ago I failed to remember. People were still passing by, laughing and talking, but I failed to see any undue excitement. I, myself, was full of nervous imaginings on the subject of what was about to happen to me. The talk to which I had listened had penetrated my mind deeply, and I was acutely aware that another experience was due shortly. In that drama I should be the star performer, but there was no indication of any other actor if Ralph was excluded.

My thoughts so engrossed me that I paid no heed to the direction in which my companion was leading me. I was dimly aware of passing houses and large buildings and was conscious that the temperature was mild and yet bracing.

In a short space of time we approached a house that was unpretentious in appearance, but spotlessly clean and free from the usual dust and grime associated with Town houses.

Ralph opened a gate giving entrance to a path leading to the front of the house. The perfume from the flowers that bordered the path reached my nostrils, causing me to sniff their scent appreciatively.

As we reached the door, it opened, and a man came forward and greeted Ralph affectionately, but in a tone of respect that gave me an inkling of the distance that must lie between them. There was no question of superior or inferior, but only that as of a pupil to an old and valued Teacher. He then turned to me and bade me enter.

We walked inside and I found myself in a room furnished well and in good taste. There was no passage, the door opened directly into the room. My new friend was apparently able to comprehend my earlier thoughts about lack of dirt, as he said with a smile, "You see we have no dirt here, so we can enter this room directly from the garden. I designed it that way, so that when the door opens you are at once a guest, without going through the formality of being announced or of being conducted to another room to greet your host or hostess. That is a great advantage when you consider our wish that our friends should feel perfectly at ease in this house".

From his point of view, I mused, there was something to be said for it, but, if it was raining, and everyone stepped straight into the room with muddy feet, it would be distinctly inhospitable on the part of the guests, anyhow.

Again that uncanny knack of being able to read one's unspoken thoughts was apparent, as he replied, smiling. "Yes, we have rain, but it is rain which is good for our bodies - those which we now have; it benefits and strengthens them, and that which is not absorbed runs off, but does not wet the road or turn it into mud, so it is impossible that any harm can be done to my hospitality by those who venture here to receive it".

These views, so directly opposite to those I had so often heard on Earth, caused me amazement. The fact of the lack of decay, predisposed the thought of decay; so if buildings failed to turn into dust with time, then life must of necessity continue. It was with these thoughts that I sat down at the request of my two friends and awaited further explanation.

Ralph then turned to our host and asked if it was possible for me to stay in this house for the purpose of ascertaining my way of progression, as it was now vitally necessary for me to have the knowledge of the gains and losses of my material life which would be given to me very shortly, as soon as I was prepared to receive it.

Upon being assured that no hindrance would be placed in my way, I requested Ralph to show me where I should go to obtain this most urgent information. He replied that all I required was rest and quietness, the other would be given to me in good time.

He then opened a door that led into a similar room to the one in which we were, and after giving it a brief survey declared it was aptly suited for my purpose. He motioned me to seat myself and then continued - "If you require me I shall be in the room we have just left, but you will stay here to obtain the revelation of yourself that will be a source of guidance to you in the life you have now entered. Fear nothing. Rest now in the assurance that all things are possible by obeying God's laws".

He gave me a comforting smile and left me.

16
Remembrances

I walked round the room rather aimlessly after Ralph had left, then feeling tired after the excitement of the meeting I had attended, sat down on a comfortable divan. Shortly I was resting the whole of my body on it as I gave myself up to my thoughts. These were still very confused, but already there were threads running through that gave them a consistency that I found strengthening to an inner conviction that some organisation, the like of which I had never known, was taking command of me and that it would be better for me to try to understand and obey the rules of it.

As I mused, I seemed to perceive a change in the lighting of the room. It grew brighter and more intense than it had been when I first entered, if that were possible, and it was certainly deeper in tone. Further it appeared to have some narcotic effect, for I grew very drowsy, but at the same time also vividly and mentally alert. My intelligence became consciously more acute and I was noting impressions with great vividness.

Suddenly, to my startled gaze appeared a picture of my early childhood with my Father and Mother. Every little detail was there; I could hear the voices of my parents speaking and my own voice answering them. There was no deception, I knew it was real, the clock had been put back and I, a looker-on, was seeing the life I had lived many years ago being pictured before me. As I gazed, it continued moving as if it were an actual living thing, and I saw all my early training and how I had reacted to it. I was impressed, how I know not, that I had once been given great opportunities to use for my future conduct, but had I, I wondered, made that use of them which would have benefited my fellow men?

It is not possible for me to record all that I saw of my life, for the whole length of it was laid before me, and I re-lived it within myself. At the time I was unable to determine how it was regulated, but it was all there; the good, the bad, and the indifferent, and what is considered to be the worst - the neglect to use purposefully the responsibilities that I should have undertaken. At the portrayal of many of the episodes I squirmed; at others I felt meaner than it was possible to describe. The good and intelligent use of my whole life was largely absent, but carelessness, rather than deliberate ill-doing, predominated. Much that I had long forgotten was brought back to me until I shouted aloud for the revelation to cease. But this self pity had no effect - I had to see, and re-live it all. At last, when the period was reached at which I had died and passed to my present existence, the picture stopped as suddenly as it had begun.

17
A New Helper

However, the whole of my tuition was not yet finished. When at last I roused myself from my humiliating thoughts I saw I was no longer alone; a man was in the room with me. He had the mien of an old wise man, yet from his youthful appearance he could have been only about forty years old. From his eyes, wisdom as depicted by ancient sages, poured out towards me like living knowledge, until I was filled with a burning desire to ask this stranger if he would help me in my extremity, and assist me to understand the inner meaning of the scenes I had just experienced.

Once again I had a demonstration of the power of thought in this new world which had so puzzled me in those cases which I had already met, who spoke without words, for I could actually feel my unspoken thoughts being received by this man. I knew that there was no room for deception, for in the same manner that I had already experienced in getting the thoughts of others, so I appreciated the fact again that my own unuttered thoughts were being heard and understood.

As this knowledge flooded over me, I gasped. Then into my inner hearing came a wise voice saying, "Why should I not give help, if the appeal is given in earnestness of mind? My friend, that is exactly why I am here. From my longer experience it may be possible for me to throw a little light upon what you have just seen, and from my knowledge, perhaps, be able to point out a way for you to unravel the threads of your life which you have so tangled. Do not think however, that I possess all knowledge and wisdom. I am a man in spirit, as you are now, but I have travelled a little further, that is the only difference. So I am allowed to advise you, but am not permitted to carry any of your burdens for you. Therefore confide your misgivings to me, and between us we shall then be able to devise a way of understanding that is in accordance with the laws of God, that you may abide by them and carry them out".

Upon hearing this, a great feeling of relief pervaded my mind and I rose impulsively and went towards my visitor. He at once stepped forward and grasped me by the hand. Until that moment I had not been quite sure that he was real, but as I felt the firm contact of his hand in mine I was at once both re-assured and comforted.

18
Recapping...

Now I will break off my personal story for awhile, as I think that an explanation is needed so that this experience can be treated as a whole. So before I go further I shall endeavour to summarise how far my ideas on material things have changed.

On my first arrival here I was certainly perplexed but not unduly perturbed, for I was bolstering up my courage with the thought that, perhaps, I was undergoing a particularly vivid dream. This I quickly proved was wrong; so it was succeeded by the idea that it was due to a violent upheaval of my imagination. Again that did not hold good for very long; and I then became imbued with the idea that perhaps I should continue to live in this new territory in a way similar to that in which I had lived during my earth life, but perhaps with slight variations. Then followed the unheralded intrusion of different personages, and the uncanny knack they all had of being able to read my thoughts before they were put into words. That gave a great jolt to my surmises, and as I have just shown, plunged me into unknown depths of bewilderment and uncertainty.

After that came the meeting in the great Hall, and the advice to which I had listened, intensified later on by my being forced to live over again my whole life's experiences.

That last episode had dispersed for good any ideas I might have held that in this new world I could escape from the failures of my former existence. On the contrary, it brought me to the full realisation of the responsibilities attached to it. It taught me that whatever had been done, I alone and no other was responsible. The good, bad, or neglectful was all of my own doing, and that the quicker I digested this truth, the better would be my outlook for my future performance of life's Duty.

Naturally, I had not arrived all at once at this reasoning; it had been attained gradually after many misgivings and doubts. But of the truth of the last part - the personal responsibility - I was vividly aware.

The arrival of this man who was able and willing to help me in my selection of the best way to nullify the mistakes of the past, and help me to fashion a life more in keeping with the one required, was a double blessing.

The manner of his arrival taught me that there were powers of transition beyond any of my conceptions. It was an undoubted fact that his appearance had not been heralded by the opening of a door, and looking at him I smiled at the thought that he had climbed walls and entered by a window. I saw clearly by looking round that the windows were undisturbed, and I knew that I had been gazing out of them, full of my own thoughts, at the very moment that I discovered he was in the room with me.

I had by now cast away all my preconceived notions of a heavenly host awaiting to hear the judgement on some sinner, and not yet knowing whether to extend a welcome, or to turn their backs until the verdict had been given.

The whole matter was in a very different category. I realised that the onus of acquiring strength of will and purpose to go forward, was on my shoulders, and I alone had the blame or the praise. So the sooner I received more enlightenment, the more able I should be to unravel the knot of disillusionment I had bound about myself. My only hope of getting a true focus was to accept what I saw and heard for the time being, and later arrive at a true assessment of values.

Now you must have a good picture of the state of my mind as I turned to give my attention to my visitor.

19
My New Counsellor

He introduced himself as a Counsellor, but gave no other inkling as to his identity. I was perfectly satisfied to leave the matter there, having no desire to probe further. That could wait. What was of real and abiding interest to me at the moment was the meaning he was prepared to give me about my dubious material life, which was now my only great concern.

He had a strong voice that gave his words the full vibration needed to impress me as to his fervour and sincerity. "Yes" he repeated, "I am able to instruct you in the meaning of many things you have witnessed since you have been here; that is, of course if you are willing to listen. For you must learn that you are still able to refuse to listen, or to participate in anything, in the same way as you could have refused in your previous existence. Your health, career, or financial prosperity is not at stake now; only the realisation of the true meaning of life is at issue.

"You have just seen the mistakes and failings of your previous passage through the life of your world; how little use you have made of the many gifts that God had given you. God gave them to you, not for your own gratification, but to be used to lighten the passage of others - those whom you neglected instead of assisting. I need not go into the full history of that, you have been made aware of it all. Your concern is now as to your future.

"The provision for your sojourn here is exactly in accordance with the value of the good you have been able to give to others. That is the only criterion that counts. What love and understanding have you shown for your fellow travellers? That will be seen in the kind of habitation you will be given, for it is from those acts that the material is received for the building of your home.

"God gave Man the free will to use or misuse his gifts; He is then asked for forgiveness! What has He to forgive? Each individual alone has carried out their own purposes, and left Him entirely out of them. It is only when people discover the results of their waywardness that they ask for forgiveness. It would be far better and more practical to ask those that you have hurt or offended for their forgiveness, and then you may be able to appreciate the love of God for all his creatures.

"He has designed all things for the ultimate good of all his children, not only for those who endeavour to escape the penalties of their own acts, but also for those who have never craved mercy or forgiveness. It would indeed be an unjust law if the personal responsibilities of man should escape its reward - good or bad - by calling loudly for preferential treatment. Nay, it is only by well intentioned acts that the true weight of right intentions can be calculated.

"Your own value has been weighed on such scales as I have depicted, and if those scales have tipped one side against you, who but yourself placed the adverse weights there? God gave you eyes to see with, and ears to hear; but you neither saw nor heard His request that you should do unto others as you would

that they should do unto you. These words may have a familiar
ring, but I am very certain that you see a new truth in them now!

"Well this is enough to show you how the balance has
been arranged, and how it can be adjusted if you will it.

"I shall now draw your attention to matters nearer at hand.

"To be actively concerned in the fulfilment of your life
you must consider all the events and actions of your previous
existence. Then you will be better able to comprehend the
reason for the portraying of your earth life. That has just been
done in your case, and now comes the period of meditation, to
be followed by suitable action if you consider such a course to
be advisable.

"You can, if you wish, refrain from doing anything at all
and await the results of your tardiness. It is not for me to say, but
I strongly recommend progressive action".

With these solemn concluding words ringing in my ears,
my strange companion left me. Again no opening or closing of
the door, but just - disappearance.

20
Support From Ralph

I now felt that I had stayed long enough in the room where any ideas I might have once had of escaping from my own exposure had been taken from me, leaving me fully aware of all my shortcomings, so I went out by the door through which I had entered.

I found Ralph in the outer room, and after giving me a searching look, he came towards me saying, "The experience in there", indicating the room, "was necessary, but now that you have been able to review yourself as you lived your material life, I hope it will result in a better thing being made of the present one than of the previous".

He did not actually put into words what he intended me to know, but I already understood what he inferred.

"It has been a rare and mortifying exposure of my inner weakness and lack of intelligent anticipation," I admitted. "That being so, whatever lies before me is only what I have prepared for myself, so I must not expect anything beyond my deserts.

Now indeed I know that God is not mocked. It is only such persons as myself who have mocked and deluded ourselves. The punishment is prepared by us and there is no further appeal, for I instinctively know that what I am about to undergo has been deserved. Now leave me, that I can begin my penance and pain".

Ralph looked at me with commiseration as he replied, "My friend, you cannot keep me away from you, even if I have to stand aside and watch you take wilful and mistaken steps. But I shall be with you during your period of travail, not always seen, but always there. Now follow me and I will introduce you to your home and the neighbourhood in which you will reside until many things have been remedied".

21
A New Beginning

We left the house together, but before leaving I asked to see our host and thank him. But his absence was explained by Ralph saying that as he had been able to be of help to me, no thanks were needed - the act of service was sufficient.

It appeared to me that I must have been in the house for many hours, but outside, the light seemed the same as it had been when I entered. Upon mentioning this to Ralph he said, "Yes, you have been in there for a long space, for much has been crowded into that time, therefore it seems long. But to us who waited, it has been very short, for our space is not used in the same way as yours has been. You will have to forget "Time" as you knew it. Here, it is only measured by accomplishment. This you will more fully understand later".

As we were talking, I saw we were approaching a bridge with quietly flowing water beneath it. The bridge was another surprise to me as I had imagined such a thing would be unnecessary, and so would be absent. For, I thought, if it was possible over here to enter and leave a room unperceived, it must be just as simple, to those who knew how to do it, to cross over water without need of a bridge.

We crossed the bridge, however, in the ordinary manner, and on the opposite bank of this river or stream I saw houses. They were similar to many others I had already seen, and so created no interest. I glanced inquiringly at my companion, but as he did not speak, I refrained from questioning him as to our destination.

There were people walking about, and we had already passed a number on our journey, but they had all seemed to be quite indifferent as to our meeting and passing them.

Now we entered a more imposing thoroughfare having shops. I looked into the windows with interest, but they all appeared to be very dusty and most unpleasing. I endeavoured to discern some reason for the differences from the usual attractive displays generally shown in such shops, but could only think that their owners were lacking in enterprise; apparently they were not eager to attract customers. Then why keep their shops open, I wondered, if they were so indifferent? I was unable to find any satisfying answer.

Another cause of surprise to me was the total absence of all vehicular traffic. Carriages, coaches, and such similar conveyances, usually drawn by horses, were conspicuously absent. It was very evident that they were not used herein the manner with which I had been acquainted. No longer could animals be called beasts of burden, for if anything had to be pulled or pushed, it was being done by the person most concerned, otherwise, it was plain that the coach or cart remained unmoved!

All the people we met looked dispirited and without ambition; aimless in their manner and movement. The whole aspect of this section of the town suddenly made me apprehensive of the probability that this was the place in which I had to reside. I was shortly to be confirmed in my fears.

We now turned into a small street, and approaching a dingy house which, judging from its look had been neglected by its owner for a long time, went up the few steps to its door. Ralph turned the handle and we went inside. First there was a dark hall which we traversed, and then entered a room overlooking the street. I gazed about me with a sick feeling, this I felt assured was to be my home. I looked appealingly at Ralph.

"Yes" he said gravely, "this is the house you, yourself, have prepared for your home-coming. All has been done that was possible with the few good things in your life that you have done. Some of those have been used to reclaim a tithe of the books and other articles you have cherished, so there was nothing left with which to brighten or furnish this house. The previous tenant has gone, and having no further use for it, was willing for you to live here as long as you deem it fit for your use".

He paused and then added, "I must leave you now, but whenever you require me, remember I shall always be near to listen and assist you within the means in my power. Do not imagine this is Hell; there are other places far worse. It is just the neighbourhood in which you will find associates of a like degree to yourself: that is why you are among them. There is no need for you to stay here if you will only make provision to entitle you to enter a brighter place. The whole matter is entirely in your own hands to improve or not. You can advance if you will.

He then turned and walked out of the room, leaving me with feelings that were indescribable.

I sank into a chair, overwhelmed at the poverty of my condition, feeling utterly helpless and hopeless. Yet running through my dismal thoughts was the meaning of Ralph's words - that I need not stay here unless I wished. At once came the determination to find a way - some way - out of my awful plight as soon as possible.

I made up my mind that I would go over the rooms in this house to discover what they contained. After that I would go out and ascertain from my neighbours their own thoughts on the subject of their present condition.

As I was about to rise a painful thought struck me. I was suddenly aware that I had had nothing to eat since I had arrived in this strange new land. Why had I not thought of that before. I pondered, for I must have been here for several days, yet I was actually in no need of food! As I realised this fact I sank back again into my chair, once more a bewildered and sadly puzzled man. Another problem to be solved, I supposed, to add to the many others that still remained unsolved!

22
More Cogitations

The survey of the house did not take long; there was nothing to be seen that interested me. It was not even properly furnished, only a few odd and useful chairs and a table or two were to be seen. The whole place was murky and appeared to have a resigned and rather dissolute atmosphere about it - that is if houses can really give off a dissipated look.

To say that I was disappointed, was a mild way of explaining my feelings. The only room that seemed faintly habitable was the one I had first entered, and that was because a few of my books and other odd articles which I had discarded whilst in my former existence were there. Evidently, although they were of no practical value, they were all that I had subscribed to my future residence.

What an awful fault, that only that which is of no use had to be pressed into service to be utilised, when a man so impoverishes himself by his own actions - or lack of action while in his earth-life! In the same way apparently, if I had money here it would be of no use. In the world I did at least have a financial strength; but that had brought me nothing up here.

But why then I queried, are there all those shops here if cash has no value? Undoubtedly there were lots of things for me to learn, so the quicker I commenced my investigation the sooner some, at least, of the answers would be obtained.

During this dreary soliloquy I had been looking out of the window into the dingy street. A few people had passed but they appeared too indifferent even to glance in my direction; even their walking was aimless. I looked down at myself, and it seemed to me that I, also, had acquired that same faded appearance, for there was nothing bright about me. The realisation gave me a shudder of disgust, and to overcome it I quickly walked out into the street. My feet involuntarily turned towards the direction in which I had seen the shops. This seemed to be the most suitable place to which to go to get some answers to my questions. The thought of food also quickened my interest in getting someone to answer my enquiries.

The first shop I reached contained an accumulation of old and dusty furniture, and was apparently owned by a man who stood at the door, watching my approach. I stopped as I reached him and said, "I am a stranger in these parts and I should like to know where it is possible for me to get food and a reasonable place in which to sleep, but as I no longer have any money can you direct me to anyone who can assist me?"

The man looked at me and replied, "If you did have money it would not stay with you, for here it just dissolves into dust; it is of no use. Why do you think you need food and sleep? Haven't you been without these things for sometime now and not noticed any ill results? If it is help you want, you must assist yourself before you ask it of others".

He spoke dispassionately, but there was a slight smile on

his lips as he replied to my question. "If you are really a stranger which I doubt, for I have seen you here before, come inside and let us discuss the matter".

He stood aside as I entered the shop. The interior was certainly cleaner than the outside, and I felt a feeling of relief at being therein. We both went into a back room which was cosily furnished, and with a sense of alleviation I sank into a chair at one side of the table, while the shopkeeper sat on the other side.

Rather hesitatingly I began, "You say that I have been here before, but I have no recollection of ever being here. Maybe it is chance resemblance that has misled you, for I can assure you that everything here is very strange to me. Any information you can give me will be most welcome, as it may assist me in getting my whole outlook brightened. It is not my wish to stay in such a neighbourhood, and the quicker I can get away, the more pleased I shall be to do so".

23
A Step Forward

The man listened to my outburst with kindly interest, and then explained the reason for my being where I was at the time. It coincided with what I had already been told previous to my reaching this locality. He added details which amounted to the fact that if I was decisively determined to get out of my present predicament, I could do so after a period of struggling and climbing.

It all came to this point - that I had had the opportunity on earth to use whatever means I had possessed, both materially and spiritually, to make the world better for my having been there. If I had not done it on the Earth-plane, well, later on I should have to do it; but then it would be under more adverse conditions.

The people with whom I was now mixing were those who had omitted doing anything to brighten the lives of their fellow beings. They were not "bad", in the accepted meaning of this word, but they had lived their lives concerned only with themselves and their own convenience and comforts. Thus, they had brought over with them the same feelings to their new position in this life, and were thoroughly upset at the loss of their creature comforts. But not being able to see their way and strive to overcome their handicaps, they went about bemoaning their loss and expecting someone else to supply them with the necessary means to revert to their former state of comfortable selfishness. Formerly they had outwardly obeyed all the customary conventions so that nothing could be said openly against them. But they had never been able to appreciate that assistance, both by words or deeds, could have been given to others who needed it.

With regard to their money, it was now of no value. It had been a physical possession and so could not be kept. As they still desired it so strongly they had created some; but they were self-deluded, for as soon as they had their desire the money crumbled away. It was indeed a mirage! Neither was there any need for food and sleep, as not possessing a physical body, these once-considered necessary adjuncts to life were not needed. Being now an etheric or spiritual entity, all the sustenance for the care of such could be obtained from the etheric currents which surrounded this world.

It appeared, I learnt, that all that was necessary could be obtained by the creation of a thought which, if strong enough, would bring the desired thing into being. It was not unlike the thought that planned many things on earth, but there physical action followed. Here a different action was needed. I was also taught that even while we were undergoing our earth experience, persons are conducted to this world during sleep, in order that they may see what things they are preparing for their future habitation. This is done to spur them on to greater efforts. But unfortunately when they awake all is forgotten by the majority. With some, however, there is an urge to go forward and do some particular action, although the reason for so doing is unknown.

It was in this manner that I was first seen and became acquainted with the man to whom I was now listening, although in my case, unhappily, whatever advice he had then given me had gone unheeded.

Many of my former doubts were cleared up and thrust away, for I was determined now to use the information I had been given to its fullest advantage. The difficulty of procedure still seemed to me to be almost unsurmountable, but hoped that perhaps instruction in that might be given me later.

I expressed my doubts to this man, wondering all the time why he stayed here, if he knew the way out. It was bad enough here, although it was a palace in comparison with my dreadful house, to which I supposed I should have to return. He sensed my reluctance,

"If you would care to stay with me," he suggested, "you would be welcome and it may perhaps help you in your will to win through. It is necessary for me to stay here, but in a future period I may be able to explain the reason to you. For the present you must curb your curiosity and let me be your guide and friend while you are here".

As he spoke a peculiar smile flitted over his face causing me to think that I must be better acquainted with him than I was aware. I had a sense of having met him elsewhere, but had forgotten the occasion.

I gladly accepted his offer and expressed my appreciation, adding that it was very certain that he did not suffer from the same failing as my neighbours, otherwise he would not have offered to help me.

A kindly smile was his only explanation.

As I had nothing of value to rescue from the house I had so recently left, it was agreed that I should enter into possession of one of his rooms forthwith.

As I rose, he said, "It is necessary for me to go and visit other denizens of this district. If you would care to accompany me, I think the instructions you will hear during the visits will be of benefit to you. We will close this door and go now, otherwise we may miss some of the people with whom I particularly wish you to talk".

As he was speaking he put his words into action. He closed the door and we proceeded along the street.

24
The Other Side
of the Coin

The street was as dreary as when I had first seen it; nothing exhibiting anything of interest to awaken the senses; just drab monotony. I sighed as I looked at it, a sigh which must have been audible to my companion.

He looked at me with sympathy and said, "Your first lesson - if it can be called that - is now about to begin. Bear in mind that while you are helping others you, yourself, are being helped to get away from here; while you teach, you are being taught - knowingly or unknowingly - so bear up and do your best".

We turned into a house and without any audible sign given of our intention to the inhabitants - if it had any - walked through the door. From the outside appearance of this house it would not have been surprising if it was empty and had been so for years. It did not strike me as being in use at all. All the houses I had formerly known had always had their own personality to a certain extent, and it had then been possible for me to have some idea of the household before I met them by the appearance of their homes, externally or internally.

We had only proceeded a few steps when a voice called out. "Is that you, Albert?" My companion answered in the affirmative and shouted out that he had brought a friend with him.

It was a woman's voice, and I looked expectantly towards the direction from which the voice had come. Apparently my friend knew his way, for he opened a door and we entered a badly furnished room.

A woman, a little over thirty years of age, as far as I could judge, was seated at a table with her face cupped in her hands, the picture of apathy and lost hope. If there had been any brightness in her eyes, she might have been described as being beautiful, for her features were regular and well proportioned.

Upon seeing us she instinctively endeavoured to smile, but it was such a ghastly imitation that it would have failed to deceive anyone who hoped to receive a welcome. My companion asked her how she was, and whether she had gained any encouragement from her visit to a nearby place of entertainment.

While she was speaking it was very clear to me that she had received a good education, as her voice was well modulated and her words articulated in a manner that denoted this.

Her answers were as indifferent as her manner, betraying not the slightest interest in what had been said to her, nor in what she was saying in reply.

Such a state of apathy in one so young caused me great uneasiness, for how could the inner person be reached through such a disconcerting exterior.

I noticed that she was examining me with great care, then abruptly breaking off what she had been saying, she turned to me.

"Are you another of them who are trying to find a way out of this sort of life?" she asked. "If you are, I can tell you now that it was very easy to get here, but that you cannot leave. I have tried. A little while ago I made up my mind to escape, so I crossed the bridge; you know, the one you came over. Well, I reached the other side and thought I was free. But as I tried to go forward in the opposite direction to this place, I felt that I was being pressed back. It was not done by anything I could see; it was the air, or something that I was unable to combat. My head spun and pains shot all through my body. The only way to obtain relief was to take a step backwards. This afforded ease at once. I fought against this feeling of pressure, but it was useless. I was forced to retrace my steps over the bridge, and upon reaching this side again I was at once quite well and comfortable. So if you wish to get away, my advice is to find some other road out".

This was said in such a sneering and patronising tone, that I flushed with resentment. She noticed this and laughed loudly at my discomfiture.

"Whatever your experiences have been, I can readily imagine they were well deserved," I answered angrily. "But I am given to understand by this gentleman who is with us, that there is another way, and I am willing to try it whenever he feels sufficient confidence in me to point it out".

A petulant look and a sneer was all the answer I got to this effort of mine. I looked rather despairingly at my friend who consoled me with a smile. "There is no need for dismay because one effort has failed," he said. "You will find that if your purpose is firm enough, a setback will only spur you on to greater efforts".

"With the consent of this lady, I will try to point out the benefit of the experience she has undergone. It is well for you to bear in mind that she had an earth life that has practically brought her nothing in the nature of self-reliance. She had all her whims gratified in every manner. Men ran after her, and she chose from among them those best able to gratify her senses and physical desires.

"She blindly imagined that this sort of life would continue for a long time, and that she would have amassed sufficient wealth to be able to hire similar services after her beauty and feminine appeal had gone. But she never foresaw that another aspect had to be considered - that of God's purpose in sending her into the World. That, she never gave a thought to and so, when she was returning from some festive ball, a call came for her to pass into another phase of life. An accident occurred. She came here, but her companion who was sadly injured remained in the World.

"Upon her arrival here she underwent the same scrutiny of her past as you did, and was then guided to this place. An opportunity was given for her to consider the whole question of living a life of use or - otherwise. She has chosen the latter so far.

"After having been in this place for a long period, it was decided by those who know of these things, that an effort should be made to awaken the better part of her nature, in order that she might be able to rise above her present sordid conditions. After this has been tried, if there is no response, it is possible that she may be sent to a district which is even more degrading than this, for there are many who are preparing themselves, by their apathy and disinterest in higher things, to go to such a place. There they will meet utter darkness which you would usually describe as 'evil', and then they will have a still harder fight to escape, or they will succumb to it.

"This they will continue to do until they rise above it or go deeper. Then the longer and the more fearful will be the struggle to get out. They will eventually emerge only when the power within themselves is strong enough to seize the helm and guide them to warmer and more hospitable shores.

"You may wonder how I know this. It is because I myself have been to those depths, and am now fighting my way up to the place where it is possible to be happy once more. When you meet active evil or darkness, then indeed there is only One who can assist you. Then you need God's help in all its strength to lift you up once more.

" At this time I am not going to enlarge on all I have undergone, but it would be well if you gave thought to my words. Now, perhaps, you may have a slight appreciation of the reason why I took you with me to visit this woman".

As he finished, a look of determination settled over his features and it was very easy to understand the strength of will-power that lay within him. He asked if I was still willing to assist him, or if I was still more concerned about myself than other people.

I must admit that I had become very interested in these two people and at once signified my willingness to help in any way that he thought would be right.

His answer to that offer considerably quashed any feelings I might have entertained of my superiority; for he at once frankly told me that my own case was nearly parallel with that of the woman, the only difference being that I had not been here as long as she had. I was badly shaken at hearing from him of my real condition, and was quite unable to reply.

"If I appear to be hard", he said understandingly, it is only to clear away any self-deceit you may be harbouring. For if that deception is retained it will be found to be a big defect later on and would cause you much regret. So it is far better to throw it away at the commencement of the climb, in the same way as you would discard unnecessary luggage prior to a physical effort.

"This lady is in your own grade or position here, therefore she should be your first concern, so that if your efforts to help her are successful, she should be able to accompany you on your journey; but this time it must be by the right road. That road can only be shown to you, when by your own endeavours you have made this place more pleasant for your having been here.

"That, as you must realise can only be accomplished by alleviating the pangs of despair and sense of loss in those around you. Then when you have raised up those who will be able to continue their progress after you have left, a messenger will be sent who will lead you elsewhere. You will be left in no doubt when this One is approaching, for you will feel that it will be impossible for you to live here any longer. That is the sign for all who are to change their abode for good or - the other. It might be termed 're-incarnation', but is really only another incarnation in the law of life".

25
Preparing for a Decision

To say that I was practically ignorant of the theory of incarnation would be untrue, for I had vaguely heard people discussing it; but that was the extent of my knowledge, so this announcement left me unperturbed. I was beginning to recognise my own limitations as far as the new world I was now in concerned me. The thought that I had to make a real impression on this woman before I could get away from these present conditions, filled me with apprehension.

I gave her a quick look to ascertain if she had shown any further interest in our remarks, but she appeared even more listless and disinterested than before. Then the thought entered my mind of how alike I had been to her in the world, when anyone had spoken of anything that was outside my orbit of interest at the moment. Undoubtedly, the similarity in this respect was shattering!

I looked at my male companion and again I was vividly aware that he was correctly following the course of my thoughts, and that he was unable to find much difference between us. This caused me more mental unease, but it also forced me to be grimly determined to rise above such an attitude of mind.

It must have been this decision that made me speak again to the woman. I said, "I am no better than you are, and it is undoubtedly a bad overture to our possible companionship for me to say that we can help one another to overcome the handicaps that we are both carrying at present. To begin with, I haven't the knowledge to be able to teach or preach to you, I am badly in need of all that myself. But as we are both in the same trouble, I suggest we pool our misery; we may then be able to see a way out. It has persistently been drummed into me that if I am strong and determined, I shall find the means to get away from here - I mean, allowed to go freely, not just a question of escape and pursuit. So perhaps if you are willing to listen and endeavour to put up with me for a time, we should be able to do something, surely. The most essential thing I imagine is for us to collaborate. If you are willing, then so am I".

As I finished speaking, I noticed a slight look of interest creep into the woman's eyes. A silence ensued that seemed as if it was never going to be broken. After a long period of waiting, I had begun to turn despondently away, when her voice caused me to halt and look at her again.

At first the meaning of what she was saying failed to penetrate my mind. But after listening for awhile it was clear that she was striving to focus her mind and thoughts into a suitable reply. Her whole speech was so halting and lame that it was only with difficulty that I perceived that she wanted me to stay and listen to her, but was unable to make the effort without reviling me.

It was a curious situation to be in, for obviously this woman - whom I now learnt to have been the wife of my other companion

- had thought that I was a person who had originally come only to divert myself with the sight of her misery, and at the last minute had changed my mind, and now wished to be friendly.

Her husband who had remained silent during this exchange of thoughts, now spoke. "Don't you think it would be better if both of you were to go with me to a place where you may be able to find a common interest? There is a musical festival and plays being conducted, not far from here. They are certainly not highly valued by some of the residents, but it might enable you to become better acquainted with each other. If you will accompany me, I shall be glad to show you the place where they are held, and then leave you to your own devices".

This, on the face of it, appeared a better proposition than staying alone with this woman, and upon hearing her give an assent, I joined in the acceptance of the offer.

We all left the house and walked a short distance to a Hall. Outside of this I saw there were bills announcing the names of those artistes who were appearing, but as I was unacquainted with any of the names shown there, I passed them without further notice. Mary Smart, however, was more keenly interested, and apparently knew something of the actors and actresses for she seemed to unfreeze a trifle, saying that she had known one or two before they had died.

We entered the large entrance leading to the Theatre itself and instinctively I hesitated with the vague idea of paying for our admittance. There were the usual box-offices, but no one was in them giving out tickets or receiving money. This was just as well, for I was without money. Of the whereabouts of the little I had brought with me I was, at the present period totally unaware.

I glanced back and saw other people walking in and failing to pay, so I concluded it was the right thing to do and that the show was free.

Upon reaching the interior I found it rather noisy due to the talking of the audience and the tuning-up of the orchestra. The theatre was dull and dingy, even the upholstery looked faded and neglected. We obtained seats in what I should have described as the Stalls, and then I noticed the absence of my male companion. Upon commenting regarding his absence to Mrs. Smart, she idly supposed he had been left outside, but she was totally indifferent as to whether he put in a belated appearance or not. I then remembered that he had stated that he would only show us where to go, and then leave us. This solved for me any mystery about his absence.

I am very fond of music and good acting, but what I saw can only be described as very low in the scale of artistry. The music was played in a very half-hearted and listless manner. Its beauty being totally destroyed by the inertia of the musicians. As for the acting, it is better to say that it was 'poor' and leave it at that.

My companion, on the contrary, appeared to experience a great delight in what she saw. During the interval I asked her opinion of the Play. She answered quite coherently, admitting that it had greatly enlivened her and that she was looking forward to the second half. She insinuated that she would like to come here again if I would make arrangements for us to go together.

I now considered it an opportune moment to ask if she was able to tell me how I could be of practical assistance to her. Apparently sensing from my demeanour that I was in earnest in my proposal, she answered after some deliberation, "You may not be aware that we are now only in the anti-chamber to higher - or lower grades of existence. We are here because we have never done anything that has not been selfish, and have only refrained from downright evil things from the same motive. Therefore we have now to make the decision, the same as all the rest of the people in this sphere, as to whether we go down or up.

"I have been waiting, undecided, for some time; now I feel the moment is approaching when I shall be forced to arrive at a decision. This is causing me great fear, for I really wish to experience physical lusts, yet if I do so it will mean practical extinction for a long time. I know, too, that I shall soon tire of those lusts as I have always done. Then how shall I have the power to leave them when they become as dead ashes in my mouth? Shall I then go lower and lower to sample even more elemental things, until I become simply bestial?

"On the other hand, if I endeavour to leave here and go into a brighter country, shall I be so unused to it that I shall find no enjoyments of the kind for which I am craving; the kind which has been the mainspring of my whole life up to the present period? I must declare very shortly on whose side I am. God's or - the devil's?".

Her eyes shone brilliantly, and her body shook with emotion as she spoke and I could see the intensity of her feelings. If she had not been alive before in an emotional sense, she certainly was now!

My own feelings were under better control. That may have been because I had made my own decision a short time previously. I fully intended to get away from these surroundings as soon as I could, and I certainly did not contemplate going anywhere worse than this. As I had been told frankly that I alone was responsible, and always would be, for any condition in which I found myself, it therefore followed that it was infinitely better to go up into a brighter and more interesting country than to descend into some Hell of my own making, therefore I was determined to choose the former.

I told the woman that she had far better study and understand the law of personal responsibility now. Rather than to be forced to do so, after she had multiplied her present troubles by going lower to find worse ones to add to them.

26
More Revelations

It was now approaching the time to continue the second part of this depressing performance, and the patrons were returning to their seats. My companion was eagerly looking at them as they drew near us, evidently searching for friends, and I saw her scrutiny was rewarded, as on several occasions she nodded and waved her hand to different people. Not wishing to be embroiled in any conversation with those who might be of a similar turn of mind to Mary, I carefully abstained from returning any of the salutations.

My thoughts were centred on the problem of how to change my companion's mind and impress her with the necessity of going Forward and not Back. The religious aspect of the problem did not enter into it. It was just a question - at least that was how I saw it - of moral cowardice on my part if I failed to recognise my responsibility. I had got myself into this position through the same fault, and I was determined to reverse the detrimental process that had caused it.

You may ask why I did not ask for help. But I had fully understood from the résumé of my life's history, that if I did not do something to deserve assistance, it would never be given. Words were of no avail. Deeds were the key that opened the door. It was the consequence of my own actions that I had been saddled with Mrs. Smart. If words could have been of any use then she would not have been with me now. The action demanded of me was that by my deeds I lifted her away from her apathy and despair, so that she would be able to make a better use of her continuity of life; we both sank or swum together.

What shall I say of the second half of this miserable farce that we were watching? Nothing to cause any joyous exclamation from me, or gladness from having been there! The actors were too dilatory and disinterested in their work. Pruning and preening themselves for their own petty joy, obviously indifferent to any one or anything else. If they had ever been good actors or actresses in their earth life, I knew not neither did I care. Now they were insipid and unwholesome. Yet that seemed strange to me, for always before I had found enjoyment in listening to singing and acting. I had never been a puritan in this respect, so that there must have been some unsuspected aura of despair permeating me, causing such a view to fill my mind and to give me this disgust.

Mary's opinion was opposite to mine, for when I asked her views in order to ascertain her reactions, I found that she really had enjoyed the show. I was sure that she was speaking the truth, owing to the light that came into her eyes as she spoke about it. This only caused me additional despair!

After the final curtain we left the theatre together, and there outside we again met our host. He looked at us keenly and asked how we had enjoyed the performance. I noticed that his glance lingered on me when I forcibly expressed my opinion of the whole thing. Mary, however, hardly deigned to speak to him but relapsed into her former state of listlessness. I had a feeling that she both feared and disliked her former husband for some reason I was unable to fathom.

He appeared to be entirely indifferent to her opinion of him, and was content to do us such service as was possible in our endeavour to escape from our surroundings.

As we walked together towards our lodgings, he turned to me and said seriously, "Have you not recently received a message that you interpreted as being of supreme importance to you in regard to your future destiny?"

I glanced at him in surprise, and noticing this he continued, "I mean was not your mind influenced to make some definite decision as to whether you would go forward or backward?"

I understood that once again my thoughts had been read like the pages of an open book. "You must explain to me," I said, "how it is that certain people I have met seem to have the gift of knowing what another person is thinking without their putting their thoughts into words?"

He looked at me a little sadly, and slowly replied, "Those who are capable of doing this are those who have a great responsibility. They have the power of being able to influence others for good or evil, therefore they must be very wary of how they use it. But as I am aware that you have now arrived at a decision, I am able to give you a little enlightenment."

"I had spent my own earth life in a worse manner than you, for on occasions I did deliberate ill to others, therefore that was a sin. Many of the things you have done were not done deliberately, but thoughtlessly, through the lack of knowledge, so they were errors not crimes. That is the reason that you are where you are now. I had to go further down and deeper into the abyss. May God grant you the wisdom that may prevent you having to descend to the place where I have been; a place that is actively evil, for it is the abode of deliberate wrong-doing.

"For a time I joined others in that inferno of wickedness, and again and again I perpetuated my former and fresh evils on others. Then I met one who walked unafraid through this place and its dreadful conditions. My companions often tried to vent their evil tricks and passions on him, but they were always repulsed by some power that seemed to emanate from him. Alas! I was not backward in participating in this mischief, but found I could make no headway. Then I noticed that from time to time he spoke to one or two of us, and that then they - left us.

This puzzled me, and I determined to approach him on some subsequent visit and obtain speech with him. This opportunity soon presented itself and I then asked him what he was doing here and why wasn't he afraid of the consequences. He told me that he came to help and guide anyone who was willing to leave this iniquitous place, but warned me that those he took with him would need all their courage and strength, but if they would only persevere he could promise them deliverance from their present state.

"Well, after thinking about the matter I withdrew from my companions, and this I may tell you was very hard to accomplish, for they besieged me with their vicious endeavours to make me change my mind. After great efforts I was able to resist them, then the One who had said he could guide me called upon me and appeared to be satisfied with my initial efforts to rehabilitate myself, and we left together.

"The evil things I encountered on my journey, my falterings, and fits of weakness, I will not try to describe; the thought of It fills me, with repulsion even now. My friend - for he is that now, helped and encouraged me by every means in his power, except accomplishing for me the actual ascent from the depths. When I was weak he stood beside me until I gained strength; when I faltered and even turned back he followed me until I was ready to listen to his words once more and so regain courage. When I was ill and broken down as the result of my efforts and my previous mode of life, he guided me to a Home where I could rest away from the swarms of unclean minds and spirits that still pursued me, all intent on the one purpose, to force me to return.

"The last part of the journey was the most horrible, for I had to do that entirely by myself, for my guide told me that he was not allowed to be with me in this last lap of my trial, but promised that he would be standing at the opening of the tunnel when I should emerge at the successful conclusion of my journey."

"I wept and entreated him to stay with me, but he remained firm in his refusal. It was for me, he said, to prove my worthiness to ascend, and it was for that I was now being tested. As I had wilfully descended into evil, therefore it was necessary for me to be equally strong and single-minded to get out. You see once again, that it is not words that could help me, action was the only determining factor."

"How I was ever able to overcome the last part of that journey is still a nightmare to me. When at last I was able to emerge into the country at the further end of the tunnel, I was, to all intents and purposes crazy with delirious joy. The light seemed almost to blind me, and the release from those howling friends who had tortured me during the whole of my journey, was indescribable.

"As I stumbled and fell to the ground, my friend met me once more with outstretched hands and a smile that enveloped my whole being in its love and joy. For a long period after that, I must have slept, and during that unconsciousness my friend cleansed me of some of the foulness that had clung to me. When

I awoke I found that my clothes which had been torn and filthy had gone, and been replaced by others, respectable and clean. My mind was alert and clear, and every breath I drew in gave me back my strength."

"My guide was at my side when I woke, and gave me a kind and understanding welcome. Later, I continued my progress through various places, still subjected to temptations and abuse until I arrived here. Drab as this place is, it is a veritable paradise to that which I had left or passed through."

"While on my journeyings my guide had instructed me in the way of living so that I could be of assistance to others, and I am staying here until I am capable of going further. That will only be when I have reversed many of the things I had previously done by substituting good actions in their place. That is the reason why I have interested myself in both of you.

"During my wanderings I learned that thoughts are the main-spring of all actions, so I have actively endeavoured to make myself proficient in teaching my mind to have active, intelligent, and decent thoughts."

"Later on, I found that I was able to contact other minds and thoughts. On questioning my guide about this, he told me that those who desired could converse in thought, and that words were then unnecessary. He said that those in his own district - a long way from here, always conversed in that manner. That encouraged me to persevere, and that is the reason why I can listen to, and understand your mind without speaking."

"I have now given you a brief outline of my own life. I have done so to help you, for you are indeed at the door which may lead to that place of horror which I described to you. Take heed from my example; leave that door behind you and go forward".

27
New Plans

I felt myself shuddering in sympathy with Albert's story. To say that I was racked with pain at his recital was a mild way of expressing myself, but at the same time there surged up within me a strange joy, for I knew that this man would not have voluntarily undergone all this sorrow and struggle for an illusion. That was unthinkable. There must then be a great reward to fight for judging by the way in which he had fought. Therefore, I too could participate in this reward if I went forward progressively.

I looked at Mary and she appeared to be transformed; something had at last been lit within her! She now looked to be more human - if that is the right way to describe her - than she had ever appeared before.

She noticed my look and said impulsively, "I am glad he has told us of his trials and endeavours; it has awakened something in me that makes me want to go Up and not Down. I am now ready to go with you, and if we are attacked you will find that I have the courage to endure and be steadfast".

This heartened me considerably, and I asked my friend what was the first necessity for us to be able to commence our travels.

"It appears to me," he said slowly, "that you both need a guide to advise and help you, for you both lack all knowledge of what is required of you; also there is a need for you to learn of the place it will be best for you to strive to attain. I myself am unable to tell you this or go with you, as my work is here for the time being. But I will communicate with Harold, the one of whom I have spoken, and perhaps he will make what arrangements are necessary. Let us go to our house and there we can await his arrival".

We all entered the house, and in the room where we had previously met, our host lapsed into silence and seemed to be making a strong effort to concentrate on some inner object. After awhile I saw a small bright light flash past his head; he shook himself as though he had just roused from a doze, and said, "I have spoken to the Guide to whom I previously referred and he will shortly be here to speak about your project. So let us rest comfortably until he comes".

I thought this was a good opportunity to ask him why he was so anxious to struggle on further, for from his own account this place was a haven of refuge in comparison to that from which he had risen.

He remained silent for a short time as if collecting his thoughts, and then said abruptly, "I know that I am alive - actually living - and that all that has gone before was of my own making. Therefore it must logically follow that if I was able to make for myself such an Inferno on one side, then on the other side I am capable of making a Heaven".

He paused as if slowly choosing his words, then continued. "As it is perfectly obvious that I am not now physical, so I must be spiritual, and as God is Spirit, I must be part of Him; the lesser is contained in the greater. Thus I am able to experience the joys and contentment of the Spirit and all that it entails. Then I must use any gifts I may have for the purpose of getting nearer to that degree of the Godhead from which I sprung. I have been told of the limitless opportunities of which I can avail myself when I have regained my spiritual manhood. But first, retribution is needed for the many things I have done, not simply in error but by deliberate sin. These sins can only be appeased by my helping all those I can, especially those who are wavering and uncertain as to the right way to proceed. Perhaps God may one time say that I have repaid, and let me go to a place where I shall be content; perhaps I may again meet those who have had to stand sorrowfully aside and watch my descent, even though they were full of love for me. You are different, for you have not sinned as I did. Go forward therefore, obtain knowledge and the joy of the spirit, both of you, and when you depart, take with you my freely given blessing".

28
A Special Experience

As Albert finished his speech, there was a slight disturbance at the door, and looking that way I saw that Harold was standing there. I had the impression that he had been there some little while and had heard the whole of the conversation.

He gave us all a friendly greeting and said to our host, "I am glad that you have asked me to return and advise you. I told you before that we should meet again whenever you required any assistance from me. The newcomer who is with you has not seen me before, but the friend who helped him, came to me on receipt of your message and told me of your need. This was very necessary for I have known you and the lady for a long period and shall continue to do so for a further, and as I hope, a longer space".

He came into the room and stood before us as he continued, speaking now to myself and Mrs. Smart. "I am allowed to show you something of what is awaiting you if you so desire, so that it may encourage you in your tasks".

Upon both of us assenting to go with him, he placed himself between us and said, "Do not have any fear, the ordeal is not very terrible; in fact it is extremely interesting. Close your eyes and open them only when I tell you to do so".

I looked at Mrs. Smart and saw that she was dutifully obeying his instructions, for her eyes were already closed. I therefore followed her example.

A slight dizziness seemed to overtake me, but it was so faint that I was hardly aware of it. As I was trying to determine whether it was real or fanciful, I heard Harold's voice bidding us open our eyes again and look around us.

Instinctively I turned my face towards the place from which the voice appeared to be coming. Harold stood there smiling at me, but how very different he looked now from the man to whom I had been speaking such a short time before! There he stood, majestic and erect, with a glow that shone from within him, enveloping his whole body with a subdued light. Various colours were contained in this light, giving out a charming effect. His dress seemed to be made of some material giving a perfect background to the glow, yet even overpowering this was the look of love and wisdom that was in his face, so strong that after the first glance I was forced to look away again; the spirituality was too much for me to bear.

As I turned aside I caught sight of Mary and saw that she too had altered surprisingly. Her face now reflected her great earnestness to comprehend all that was taking place. I also recognised in her someone for whom I had been searching; I felt, overwhelmingly that I was already acquainted with her, but where and when I had previously met her, eluded me.

I looked past her and saw a brightness all round us that surpassed anything I had ever seen. The temperature was warm but invigorating. I felt myself growing in stature as I drew a breath of great satisfaction. The grass and trees were perfect in condition and foliage. In the distance I could see artistically shaped houses having instead of roofs, luxuriant flowering gardens, blessed havens of rest for anyone to stay in.

Harold who must have seen the bewilderment in my face, remarked, "This is where I live. I have brought you here to see it. To do so I have had to change your conditions for a space, but unfortunately you will have to return to your former vibrations and stay there for a while. You have not travelled here in the ordinary sense in which you would understand travel. What has happened here, is that you have been taken through another veil - other than so-called death - into this fair country. You must stay near me, otherwise you will find breathing difficult and there would be a pull that you would be unable to resist and that would drag you back to your former habitation. This will not happen while I am near you, for strength has been given to me that I may show you a glimpse of some of God's loving care for His children.

29
Understanding...

I could now see the purpose of my being here, it was to strengthen the resolve I had lately made. Well, the slight glimpse I was now being given of what can be obtained by a pure effort on my part, inspired me!

I turned to Harold, saying, "It is no doubt your intention to show us more of your domain, but before you do so can you explain to us what is really necessary for us earth people to do, so that we can prepare ourselves for a place like this?"

He looked at us and smiled, and his face was illuminated by some inward joy as he answered. "It is just that you should have, Love, Honesty, and Charity fully within you; the same lesson that has been taught you for so long, yet is still being neglected or despised! It's place has been usurped by greed and malice and envy, with all its attendant evils. Here I am not speaking of errors, for although those bring their consequences they do not carry the same evil, since errors are more to be sorrowed over than blamed. It is when you come to evil that has been deliberately and thoughtfully performed, that the Law of Retribution enters so strongly.

"God forgives those who know not what they do, but even those have to learn the consequences of their acts before they can be taught further progression. The others, alas! have to repay, physically and spiritually for their sins; thus these bring their own payment. On the other hand we have the justification of knowing that men are also rewarded for their love to their fellow men. They are each given the fruits of their efforts by being allowed to pass on to a fair country where they are able to carry on their labours to an even better advantage. In their case every assistance is given to them to be able to do even more than they have previously done.

"Then added to this is the attainment of their innermost desires, whatever those may be. It may include music, art, learning, medicine, philosophy, or even such prosaic matters as gardening, building, sailing, or the hundred and one things that make up the desires of men. There is nothing excluded except that which would involve hurt or harm to others, even to birds or beasts. There is no slaughter allowed, under whatever cloak it masquerades, such as sport. I know that in this realm animals cannot die, but they can be subjected to terror, therefore that constitutes injury and is not allowed. So in these simple ways you find the means of obeying the law of God, and reserve a right to be admitted to the home that is suited to your progress and evolution".

He paused for a moment and then added, "It will be well for you to see a little more before your return, so stay close to me and we will go to one of our workshops, if 'workshop' is a suitable name for our Temples of industry and learning".

Mary at once moved up closer to Harold, and I changed my position to his other side as we started to move towards a very large building. The roof seemed to be covered with some unusual material, for the reflection from the sky made it sparkle. The sun was high, but its rays were more mellow and benign than when it warmed the Earth. I noticed too, that our footmarks in the grass were being obliterated, for as soon as we had passed it sprang back. It was a condition of perfect unison: we walking and at the same time receiving strength to continue from the very grass under our feet.

It was my first experience of a response from any vegetation that was being trodden; it was fulfilling the purpose for which it had been laid out, so the Law was not broken. Everything, yes, even animals, plants and flowers were provided for a use but never to be hurt in any way. If this could only be understood on Earth what a change there would be in the lives of men!

While I had been thus musing, we had reached the 'workshop' and were smilingly invited inside by a pleasant-looking man. He was genuinely pleased to see us; I could tell this from the quality of his greeting. He was just welcoming old friends of whom he had thought fondly and who had returned to see him after an absence. Although I felt certain that we had never met before, I found this kindliness to be the keynote of everyone I encountered; we were all accepted as firm friends.

30
A Joyous Place...

We now entered through the spacious doorway, and I saw at once that the large interior room, or Hall, was occupied by both men and women. They were all busily working, but this did not prevent them from laughing and talking. There was an atmosphere over all of joyous activity. Everyone appeared to be activated by an impulse to give of their best at whatever task they were undertaking. This fact struck me most forcibly as it was the exact opposite to what I had so recently experienced on the lower plane.

As we passed, those nearest gave us a friendly greeting but continued their occupation. Some I noticed were writing, and those Harold told us were engaged in compiling records of what work was being done in the way of literature. All the books published on Earth of a philanthropic or scientific nature, first emanated from this workshop. The thoughts and ideas were prepared here and the book written, then it was recorded so that whenever one of those whose mission it is to frequent the Earth, asked for it, or required any information about any particular subject, it was then easily available.

It was pointed out to me by one of the workers that whenever ideas or thoughts of an unselfish nature were being used on Earth the first promptings had come from the sphere in which we were now. Also, all thoughts, good or bad, it mattered not what they were, had first been instilled into the people of the Earth by those who had left their physical bodies. This brought forward from one the question of free-will. I was answered by being assured that there cannot be any hampering of free-will, as one was always free to accept or reject the thoughts given. It was action that was restricted, not thoughts. This approach was new to me, but after a short examination of the matter, I could see that my thoughts, if I so willed, could be free and unrestricted.

I next asked what the other workers were doing, and was informed that some were studying the effects of music, others were discussing and learning different methods of healing, and that some were there for the purpose of obtaining knowledge of some particular subject in which they were interested. It was really a sorting-out place where you might obtain particulars of the thing that you contemplated doing. Then, having satisfied yourself that it was truly of interest to you, and after you felt that you would be able to pursue it, you could then pass on to another Hall where that special subject was taught, practically and theoretically.

For instance, he explained, if you were determined and capable of being a messenger to Earth - going there for the purpose of recounting your experiences after leaving it - you were prepared for that object. First, those Guides were approached whose knowledge of both worlds was so extensive that they were able to judge of one's fitness to undertake the task. If they gave their consent, then you underwent a period of preparation.

A comprehensive study of the realm you were inhabiting was first given by one able to impart this information. Then a travel study was arranged so that what was to be read or spoken about could actually be seen by you. Later, questions were asked as to your real purpose of the visit to Earth. If it was found that it would not benefit those you visited, you would not been trusted with the task. If, on the other hand it would, you would have to add to your other studies the practical lesson of going with an experienced friend so that you could become acquainted with the conditions prevailing in that part of the world. After all this preparation you will be permitted to go on to the Earth plane in an endeavour to instil into the minds of those who will listen to you, the fact that you are really alive.

The reason for all this is fairly obvious if sufficient thought is given to this important matter. The teaching given to the Earth must be true and consistent. You may easily imagine the chaotic conditions that might ensue if everyone, soon after their arrival here, could run back to give, as truth, that of which they themselves were only dimly aware through their own faulty observation.

I know of course, that some of those who have not had this special coaching are allowed from time to time to return. But this is for some special purpose. These do not go to teach or perform some universal beneficial end; theirs is for some personal reason that has been allowed - perhaps to give consolation to those they love who are heartbroken at their loss - my remarks only concern the proper and recognised Messengers. These are capable of giving great knowledge to the earth, and they can obtain all the information required for this work and also the necessary protection during their visits, for there are many who would be only too glad to molest or hinder them if they were powerful enough.

Let me give you a word of warning! These undesirables frequent all the meetings on Earth that are held for the purpose of communication. If the protection is not sufficiently strong, or if the instrument is lax, these 'grey' spirits will insert themselves, and then you get distortions and wrong messages. So you see that there is an obvious duty in both worlds to be strong and always to ask for protection whilst engaged in this most important task. No doubt many more aspects of this will spring to the mind now that attention has been drawn to it.

31
More Information

The activities in this Hall, throughout the whole progress, were of the greatest interest to me. There was really no manual work as I had known it on earth. It appeared to be entirely an effort of concentration.

One young man, for instance, was arranging a compilation of the history of the world, showing its gradients in spiritual knowledge, or its decadence. He concentrated on the particulars he had before him. Then, watching him, I saw after a period of delay what he termed a graph appear. It was outlined with a border that enclosed squares containing letters, these in turn wavered up and down across the paper. I have called it 'paper', but I imagine it was something more than wood-pulp. Although the whole thing had been created before me I had not been able to fathom the process.

Later it was explained to me that Thought, if it is concentrated on any particular thing, could be formed into a material-like substance and retained in that form as long as it was considered necessary. If it was required to be altered or obliterated, the same method was again applied, and to all intents and purposes it was amended or erased.

It was pointed out however, that as nothing can be destroyed in either of the two worlds, a replica was always obtainable if desired. This led to an interesting talk about the things made on Earth, and I was informed that of everything that man had created, its replica was stored somewhere in this new world of mine. According to its merits the 'Thing' was housed, or if it was a building, was erected where it was meant to be. Thus the lowest and most degrading of Earth's houses were placed in the lowest parts of this plane, in replica. This means that in the first plane called the 'Astral', you have a representation of all the towns, cities, or other such places of the Earth. That was the reason why I had not been more startled after my transition - what I saw was so much alike to that to which I had become accustomed. It is also geographically correct, such as India placed over India, and England over England.

I now began to understand that if buildings, etc, were placed where they were in attunement, then people were congregated together in a similar manner because it was in accordance with their desires and the manner in which they had used their lives. Those, like myself, who had been dilatory, selfish or indifferent were all, very rightly, herded together. This was correct if viewed from the right perspective, for we were all alike. It was no wonder that I rebelled at the thought of going back to such a condition as that in which I was lodged; yet for sheer justice it could not be beaten. It was for me to earn my right to happier surroundings!

It would take too long for me to describe in detail all that I saw as I followed my companion and Harold to different parts of his home and country. It was very forcibly impressed on me that the rule of like to like was well emphasised here. These were happy, earnest and joyous people, intent on improving the lot of the inhabitants of the Earth, willing and able to arrange and carry out matters for this purpose. All other things of importance were left in the capable hands of those whose work, or joy, it was to carry them out. From here went forth those spirits who met those who had just arrived and shepherded them to their respective homes. Those who had passed to us through sickness were gently and tenderly conducted to Rest Houses or convalescent Temples until they had been taught how to overcome the supposed physical ailments they had brought over with them.

At these Rest Houses, doctors and nurses were in constant attendance. But here, in opposition to the usual rule that prevails in Earth hospitals and other such places, these knew that all their patients would surely recover. This knowledge must be one of the greatest joys to these earnest men and women who, in the majority of cases, were continuing the work they had done whilst in their physical bodies. What a splendid thought to them that their ministering care unto others would not be useless, but that there was not an illness that they could not conquer, and that all those they attended would be well and happy once more!

These thoughts filled my mind at the time and have remained with me ever since. For I have seen all these things accomplished in the manner depicted on many occasions since then.

32
Everyday Reality

After being made acquainted with many more matters of a similar kind, all given with the sole intention of awaking our interest, we were conducted back to our previous abode by means of Harold's protection.

Upon our return he said to us both, "You have now had a foretaste of what will be your own, eventually, so I can leave you for the present as I am sure there is much for you to talk over. When you have reached a united decision, think strongly of me and I shall be with you".

He turned and left us.

As far as I was concerned I had already arrived at a decision; it was to go forward at any cost, even if it meant that I had to carry my companion with me.

I explained this to Mary, but she astonished me by saying, "Perhaps it will be me who will have to assist you! At the present moment you are at fever heat to go forward, but I can foresee a time when you will not feel quite so valiant and determined, and then I am sure my aid will be necessary. You must remember that there are sure to be temptations to stray, and there it is that a woman's intuition will be of great use".

On pondering over this statement, I could see the common-sense of the answer, and after a further discussion we were in agreement.

I subsequently found that the plane of existence on which we were at this time, is generally known as the 'Astral'. It would better be referred to as a clearing-house, for it is the place through which all travellers pass in order to go to a lighter or darker plane. It is possible to linger here for a time, but sooner or later there is some compelling force used from outside that makes the lingerer go on.

During my sojourn here, I became acquainted with different persons who were endeavouring to continue their physical life. As they had now left their physical bodies, they made every effort to conjure them into being again. As they were only faintly successful, this type of being thronged the approaches from the Earth and did their utmost to persuade new arrivals to go with them so that their physical appetites might be appeased. Those that were stronger than their fellows prevailed over the weaker, and some even penetrated to the Earth again. There they caused as much disturbance as they could evilly devise by joining with those of a like mind who were still physical beings. This explains perhaps, why such incomprehensible things are sometimes done by humans who are not capable of controlling their own inclinations. If you desire it, there are those who are helpful who will join you, but remember the reverse is also true, a union can be made by the other kind!

I became deeply interested in all these matters and was considerably surprised at the mixed thoughts that were held by some as to where they were now. On one hand I was positively assured that I was in Heaven; on the other hand some in all earnestness told me that I was not really physically dead, but was only being prepared for a return to the world I had left; the impression being held by these people that we were gods awaiting a time to go to our kingdom.

Well, if some of those who spoke to me thus were gods and able to return, the World was due for a shock when it saw them for, judging from their ravings, the reverse was more likely to be true. Then I met others whose conversation had to do solely with gains and financial deals. They justified this by saying that 'you never knew', and that perhaps it might come in usefull. Then you can easily imagine that the whole place was a hot-pot of mixed thoughts and curious ideas.

I think I have written enough to give you a fair idea of the kind of place that is immediately about the world. It is very necessary that there should be such a place, for so many who come over to us lack all knowledge of where they are or where they are going; so until they have sorted themselves out in familiar surroundings it is impossible to make any impression on them.

You can now realise why, from this side every endeavour is made to give some information about this life to those of you we can reach, and who are still frequenting your world. Thus the necessity for staying or loitering on this Astral plane is avoided. Further, if you have some previous knowledge of your future life, your friends here can be seen by you when you join them and then, after greetings are over, they can take you away from this place of shadows to a brighter existence.

33
Starting Work

It was no longer any use for me to try to hide the fact that it was now even more necessary than ever for me to get away from this environment that I had earned, although I knew that to do so would entail a great deal of hard work and perseverance on my part.

Mary also would need all her courage and strength to go forward with me, but whatever the ordeal, it must be overcome. To hesitate now would be fatal to our aspirations, so the quicker we adventured forth, the better would be our chances.

The first part of our pilgrimage was comparatively easy, for the people we met were completely indifferent as to wherever we might be going.

Soon after leaving the town we were met by a fashionably dressed man, who, without any invitation, joined us. His conversation was witty and interesting and I gathered that he, himself, was well satisfied to be in his present position. It appeared that he thought it was better than he had anticipated, so he was delighted with it. That was certainly an entirely new aspect of the matter, and only showed how differently each person viewed their lives.

He soon left us, however, and we wondered where we were intended to go, as it was surely time our Guide should have met us.

It did not seem that we had been walking very long, or it may have been that our conversation together on the train of events that had caused our meeting, made the time pass quickly, when I noticed a man nearing us.

I observed his approach keenly, but he was an obvious stranger, and I turned my gaze away, thinking he would go past us. He failed to do so however, in fact he stopped and smilingly said, "I imagine you are waiting for me so that you may commence your work?"

I looked at him in astonishment! How could he know what we required?

"Do not be so surprised", he smiled, "I have been in communication with your friend Harold, and so I know the circumstances of your journey, and to what you aspire. As I have had some experience of the work required of you and this lady, it was thought advisable that at the commencement I stayed with you for a time and gave you the benefit of my knowledge".

Recovering from my surprise, I welcomed and accepted his offer with gratitude. I then asked him what our occupation was to be, for as yet I had no specific knowledge of it, as only comments had been made about it in a general way, so far.

Our Guide, for so I will call him, replied, "You have already been prepared in some slight manner, although perhaps unknowingly on your part. Have you not been informed by one who had been there about the darker planes and their torments and troubles? Have you not also had an experience of the place to which you were first taken, and told that it was all you had earned, and so deserved? Further, were you not carried to a higher realm and saw the beauty, orderliness and wisdom of it, before you reached this present stage of your wanderings.

This I assured him was very true, but what was the inner meaning for us that was contained in it?

He explained. "This was a necessary instruction for you both, as you were required to have a knowledge of these matters so as to learn the work needed for your upliftment. It has been decided by those who are well acquainted with your earth lives that it is vital for you to be instrumental in helping those who pass from Earth with an insufficient knowledge of their continuity of life. You will find this task to be arduous but enthralling if your determination is strong enough to enable you to undo some of the foolish things of your former existence.

"You will find that it is not always easy to convince some of the strangers who reach our shores that you are not there to bring them harm, but to assist them. You would do well to remember that some Earth children have a stronger belief in a so-called devil, than in God. Your task will be to endeavour to persuade these people that you are like them through having recently died, but that you have now been able to see, hear and absorb some knowledge of the place in which they have foregathered.

"Every effort must be put forth by you two in order that those you meet do not tarry, and you must actively oppose any others who may try to frustrate your endeavours. This will recur over and over again, for the forces of evil always oppose those of good. But you should be aware by now that the former never had, or will have, the power or strength of the latter.

"Both of you are now enlisted on the side of those who give help and assistance, so you will forgive my insistence that you should only do that which will be right.

"I shall stay with you, as I have already explained, for a short time, but later should you be so beset by those of a lower evolution that you fear defeat through your inexperience, think forcibly of me and I will be at your side immediately to render all possible assistance. It will only be through your own weakness that this can occur, so accept comfort from the thought that if you are strong there can be no overcoming of you, or your efforts made fruitless".

I gave very earnest attention to all these instructions, and so did Mary, for I saw her following our Guide's words with complete engrossment,

She then spoke to him for the first time, putting into words my own thoughts. "How are we to know the newcomers from the inhabitants? She queried.

The Guide smiled and replied, "Those who ask of you the way, or those who appear too tired and weary to go any further, or those who you find asleep on the ground, those are the ones in whom you must interest yourselves. The opposite side will very quickly announce their presence by their actions and words".

He paused, and then added, "Now that you have understood the nature of your work, it would be well if we commenced at once. You already know that there is no night to divide the day, neither do you require food for your sustenance, so the whole of your time can be devoted to this work, until the notice for your release is given".

As the Guide finished speaking, he pointed, and as we followed the direction of his hand, we saw several persons slowly climbing the brow of a hill a short distance away.

"Those are some who require our help", he said. "So let us proceed to give".

As this was to be my first experience of my new work, it was not to be wondered at that I felt nervous and a little excited.

I eagerly accompanied my Guide as he approached these new people. When we reached them I saw there were two men and a woman. One of the men was elderly but the other appeared to be comparatively young, about twenty-eight or thirty years of age I estimated, while the woman must have been between fifty and sixty. They seemed to be entirely bewildered and lost; just struggling along with no particular expectations of anything definite.

Our Guide halted in front of them and smilingly asked if he might assist them in any way, explaining that it was easy to see that they were strangers in this part of the country.

The three people upon hearing his voice huddled together and looked about them wildly. It was quite apparent that they were unable to see us, for the young man asked his companions if they had heard a voice offering assistance.

The others both answered to the effect that they had certainly heard it distinctly, but were quite unable to discern who the speaker was, or where he was standing.

This answer caused me considerable astonishment as they were perfectly plain to me and so, I thought, we should have been equally distinct to them.

Later on I was informed that some people on their first arrival deliberately closed themselves in by their own thoughts, so that although they may appear to have clear-seeing eyes, yet they are almost blind. This is usually caused by fear at what they might behold; the results of their former teaching, or, perhaps the lack of it.

Our Guide then said quietly, "You have nothing to fear, we are not going to cause you any harm but only want to help you. Why don't you compare yourselves with us so that you may know that we are just like you and that there is nothing extraordinary about us. If you will strive to do this, your normal eye sight will return and you will be able to see me, for I am standing only a few feet in front of you".

Again it was the young man who answered, "Well, there doesn't seem much wrong with that advice, but things are very strange. I can see things around me quite clearly yet I seem unable to see the one who is telling me what to do".

They then sat down and talked the matter over between themselves while we silently watched them; our Guide was with a kindly smile on his face, which gave him the look of being perfectly able to understand the whole situation.

How long we stood, silent and waiting, I am unable to say, but after some while the strangers appeared to become more composed and began to peer in our direction, shading their eyes with their hands as if slightly dazzled.

Then our Guide spoke again, advising them to continue their attempts, as they were now looking in the right direction, and success would soon reward their efforts if they persevered.

On glancing round, I now saw that a number of other people had gathered near to us and were taking a very lively interest in our proceedings.

I was not favourably impressed by these newcomers for they all had a jeering and hostile expression and the glances they turned in our direction were the reverse of friendly. There seemed to be some actual active enmity emanating from them.

Then a thought flashed into my mind, recalling the warning that had been given us that we should not be allowed to go on our pilgrimage unmolested. I glanced for assurance at our Guide, he seemed unperturbed, and from him I drew a sense of courage and comfort.

Mary, also, must have understood the menace of these later arrivals, for she drew nearer to me and took my arm as if for comfort. I thereupon held her closer and together we moved towards our Guide. He perfectly understood this, for he flashed me a quick smile and placed an arm on my shoulder. As he did this I experienced a feeling of such relief and self-reliance that I cannot ever remember having felt its kind before in the whole of my life.

Being thus strengthened I turned my attention to those three people whom we had tried to aid. I saw now that their hands had dropped from before their eyes and that they were staring in front of them with great excitement.

It was easy to perceive that now they had their eyes opened and could see us clearly.

34
Following Through

My anxiety decreased as I saw the composed and alert attitude of our Guide. He was ready and prepared for all eventualities, so I knew at once that this was very far from being his first experience, even if it was mine.

The three strangers were now examining us, as they stood and awaited our first advance. They were clearly apprehensive, but not unduly alarmed.

Our Guide, keeping us both close to him, said to them, "I and my friends with me have come to give you a welcome, and to invite you to go with us until your own friends are able to reach you. You, I know, have been lost and are still wondering in your minds as to what has happened to you and where you are. This need not cause you fear for many others are also unacquainted with this country on their first arrival, but they soon become acclimatised, and are then pleased to remain. If you will allow us to be your conductors, they, your friends, will thank us for so doing, and you, yourselves will be comforted".

I watched with breathless interest to see the effect of these words upon these lost people. The elderly man appeared to be bewildered and unable to grasp the purport of them. The young man apparently understood their meaning without an effort, for his face lit up and he spoke quickly. "If you can find and take me to Emma, that will be a grand thing for me. I don't care how far I have to travel, I will go", and he strode purposely towards us.

The woman had also understood, that was very evident as she said, "Where is the place in Heaven that has been prepared for me? Where are the angels to lead me to that place near the Throne?'

Then throwing tier arms into the air she wailed, "Where is God for whom I have given up so much and worked so hard; where is He? I know He must be near, for as I lay dying I was told He awaited me, and the Church's blessing was given to me, so I know that I am saved and that my sins are washed away".

As she concluded her speech, I saw looks of dismay cross the faces of her male companions. It was evident that this was the first intimation they had received that they had now passed over the narrow river men called "Death".

The other group of people who had gathered around us appeared to be highly amused at this outburst, as laughter and coarse remarks reached my ears. I did not turn to try and find out who might be the instigators of this hilarity, but continued to watch events.

Mary drew near to me and whispered, "I am glad that when I came across I didn't expect God to meet me, so I wasn't so badly surprised at what I found. This poor woman is in for a shock when she realises that she will have to walk towards God, and He will not come to her".

Our Guide overhearing this remark, said sadly, "This woman has taught herself to expect services instead of giving them, so there is no cause to be surprised at her agitation and dismay at finding that she is alone. It is entirely due to these peculiar ideas of sanctity, that she is so bewildered, for in her own way she has really done good with her life, but owing to her blind outlook, she is still unable to see or welcome her friends".

Then turning directly to Mary, he said, "Please go to her and assure her that she is under the same protection of God, and that if she is willing to go with you, she will be able to see the place He has had prepared for her - not by His throne - for that would only cause her embarrassment, but in a house where she may rest in reality still blind although she appears to be able to see."

Then pulling me forward, he spoke to the younger of the men, saying, "Yes, my friend, it may seem a trifle strange to you, but you have now passed through the Valley of the Shadows you called "Death". It could not have been a fearful proceeding for you, or you would have known more about the journey and would be bearing scars of the encounter! But now you hardly realise you have already crossed that river, and you are eager to find the one whom you loved and who left you. She cannot be found here, but if you will make yourself ready, in God's good time you will be able to see her and be within reach of her. Whether she will be able to speak to you, I know not, but it will be your task to convince her of your near presence, and then, no doubt the other desired accomplishment will follow. Stay for a while whilst I speak to your companion, and we will then accompany you to one who is anxiously awaiting your coming".

A shadow passed over the face of the young man as he listened, and he seemed to be in deep distress.

The elder man had also listened, but in an indifferent way to all that had been said. Suddenly he shouted out, "Who are you, that you know all these things? Are you alive or dead? You must certainly be mad to tell me that I am dead. Why I am feeling better already and much stronger. I shall soon be able to get about again. My brain only seems a trifle dizzy, and when that clears I intend to go out and do whatever I want to, and nobody, madman or any other, is going to stop me".

This speech gained great applause from the onlookers, and such remarks as "quite right too; do exactly as you want, don't be led astray by fools" were shouted across to us.

The crowd pressed even closer on us, and appeared to be heartening themselves for an attempt to get between us and those to whom we were speaking.

Our Guide gave no sign that he had heard the remarks, or if he had, was not interested. All his attention was focused on the man in front of him. He spoke to him again, earnestly reiterating his request that the stranger should come with us, and vouching for his safe custody on the journey.

This plea gained no further response as far as we were concerned, but the man slowly turned towards those of the crowd who were nearest to him and asked if he might join their group.

This request was welcomed with glee, and many hands were thrust forward to help him towards their ranks.

Our Guide made a last effort; he waved back the people and they retreated a little and quietened. Again speaking directly to the elderly man he said, "You do not understand, and so cannot realise the responsibility you are undertaking in asking that you may go away with these people; if you did, you would be fearful of the results. They are only endeavouring to entice you away from your purpose, which is to find those who love you and will care for you. If you do go with them, as you have requested, it will be a very long time before you can reach this part of your journey once more. Owing to your strong endeavours in the life you have just left, it is justifiable for you to go Forward, and join your loved ones. God, however, only requests you to go the right way, He leaves it to your own will to accept or refuse. He allows me to point this out to you, but that is all. If you wish, I can force these people back, so that your forward journey is unimpeded, but I cannot compel you to accompany me".

This speech seemed to impress the man, for he looked on the ground as if in deep consideration. After a short pause he turned to his male companion and said, "I don't believe he can do all he claims to be able to do, and surely all these other people cannot all be wrong. So if you are willing to go with him, I shall be leaving you".

With these words he walked into the midst of the crowd, and I saw him speaking to some of them.

Our Guide gave a sigh of compassion and said, "How often it happens that the matter that receives the most notice and applause is vociferous and so is considered the finest. Yet some small thing, of such supreme delicacy that it has to be hidden so as to save from hurt - is left, because no effort is made to find it. That is what the unfortunate man has done. The tender love that is awaiting him a little further on must languish unseen and unrequited, owing to his weakness in being unable to distinguish between the real and the false. You will have many disappointments in this way, but always remember that eventually those you may deem lost will travel this way again, repentant but full of hope".

He then walked towards the younger man, and the woman to whom Mrs. Smart was speaking. "You two need not fear to accompany me", he said, "for those that desire to greet you are greater than those who would hinder your progress towards your loved ones".

The people in the crowd nearest to us again began to call to the two, advising them to leave us and join them, and some of the foremost became very threatening, as though they would stop us by force. There appeared to be two or three more violent than the others and these continually urged others forward. They seemed imbued with a very lively dislike of our Guide judging by the manner in which they shook their fists at him, and the epithets they shouted.

Now, as though his mind was fully made up, our guide took the arm of the young man and of the woman, and telling us to follow closely behind him, he walked towards the more violent of the group I have described. It seemed that our way through this crowd was to be disputed, and I could not see how it was to be accomplished against such superior numbers.

This matter, however, did not seem to disconcert our leader, for he went steadily forward. Then I saw to my surprise that a bright light, was emanating from him. It grew wider, and I saw with fascinated eyes that it was spreading around all of us and was illuminating our whole company. I experienced a feeling of warmth, followed by one of great confidence. Then the meaning of the words recently said, those that are with us are mightier than those who are against us", came to my mind with a greater force and a clearer meaning than I had ever recognised before!

The effect of this light on those who were opposing us was remarkable! It seemed as if they were being scorched by a fire that threatened to incinerate them if they stayed where they were. The violent and the strongest ones were affected most, for they cowered away affrighted, and as soon as they considered they were safe from the effects of the light, they turned away and ran!

A way was very quickly opened before us, and from the expressions on the faces of those we passed, they appeared to be relieved and glad to see us go.

We continued our progress until we had moved out of sight of the crowd who stared after us but did not attempt to follow. We halted and I drew a breath of relief. Then I noticed that the wonderful light that had made our advance possible had gone again.

35
More Answers

The tranquillity that ensued was very refreshing after the clamour we had just left, and allowed us time for calm reflection. What, I pondered, was the origin of the wonderful power that apparently poured out from our Guide, and that created a passage for us through the hostile crowd? Why was it that they were not more actively opposed to us instead of satisfying themselves with mere shouts and curses? Why were they so anxious to encourage the elder of the men to go with them and not with us? What should I have done if I had been left to them by myself?

These were only some of the thoughts that flooded my mind as I looked back. Then, once more that power which is so developed over here, of hearing and seeing thoughts as concrete things, came into force again. Shall I ever get over my amazement of it, I wonder? As our Guide said, "I will endeavour to answer those thoughts of yours which are so disturbing you.

"To begin with; that light or power which you yourself really only saw faintly, because it was far brighter and stronger than you imagine, came from some friends of mine who collaborate with me in this work. You have heard it said that the Hosts of God are stronger than the workers of evil if you will but ask for their aid? Well, this was a practical demonstration of it! I asked of God for help and comfort in assisting those who were endeavouring to go the right way as far as they could determine. This appeal, like all such appeals sent out for the help of others, was at once answered in all its force by my friends standing beside me, unseen yes, but very soon felt as you noticed.

"Those of our opponents who appeared to be most active in pressing others to attack us, were able to see and appreciate the power that was arrayed against them. You noticed, I think, that they took care to keep in the rear of their dupes, and as we approached them, they fled. They had had previous encounters in which they had been worsted, so they were riot prepared to stay and receive the effects of our nearer advance. They knew that if they had, they would have been scorched and hurt, not physically of course, but in their nerve centres - their whole being; for evil cannot stand before the power of God's spirit. If it is attempted, then their spiritual life is treated like a moth fluttering round a candle, they are singed and hurt. Now you can understand the reason for their hasty retreat.

"In this case it was arranged that we should meet the wanderers a little distance past the points from where they had emerged, and not within the precincts of the town you have lately left. This was done so that your first encounter should be equal to such an onslaught. You must remember that God never gives you more than you can carry. If this meeting had taken place in the town, or further on, it would have been more violent; an active hostility, as you would term it, would have been met because more of the violent and strong element would then have been backed up by the denizens of the lower planes, all eager to snatch a spirit away from our guardianship.

"You may believe me when I say that in that case it is a dangerous position for anyone to be in, if they lack confidence in God's power to overcome all evil. But in this particular case all the element of evil in its fullest conception was lacking. What took place was really more of a temptation in order to create fear within you, than an active evil. Happily you did not allow fear to enter, so you and your companion were incapable of being harmed".

"With regard to your query as to what you would have done in this case, that is rather unnecessary I imagine, for you appear to have forgotten that I was here specially in order to show you what will be required in the future, so I will at once assure you that if you unswervingly do that which you have been asked to do, the powers that you have just seen exhibited will always be yours when they are required. The thought of being unable to accomplish that which God has given you to do should pass right out of your mind, never to return".

He paused, and as I looked into his kindly and intelligent face, I knew I was listening to one who simplicity believed in the power of God and its capacity to overcome all evil.

A sigh went up from beside me, and turning I saw it emanated from Mary who appeared to be just waking up from a beautiful sleep. Her face looked brighter and younger than I had ever seen it. The dissolute and faded look had gone! It had been replaced by one of determination and joy.

She impulsively grasped my arm and half whispered, "It is all truth that he has told us, for I felt the power of those friends of whom he speaks, enter my whole being. An internal war was at once provoked through my lack of being able to distinguish between good and evil. But after that had subsided and I asked to be allowed to do all I could for the right, I seemed to change.

An assurance of God's power pervaded me, and without any tremors I stayed on and had no wish to go back with those who were tempting me. Yet it is only a short time ago that I thought I should want to stay there for ever.

"Previous to this, I had little faith in our efforts to be able to leave the town, but now I know we can do so if we but do that which this man tells us to do. He speaks with authority and great power, so it is best for us to accept his advice and go with him until we are able to do by ourselves what he has done".

She ceased and turned away, going again to the woman whom she had been helping along the road.

36
Continuing the Learning Process

Now I really understood the change that had taken place in this woman, it was a spiritual one, for she was now prepared to go on regardless of consequence to herself if she could but do good for others. She had learnt the greatest lesson of all, the one that has always been taught but very rarely understood or carried out.

I felt a little shame faced when I considered my attitude. I saw it was one more of curiosity to find something better for myself than, as it should have been, one of giving help. This I earnestly assured myself should be remedied and I at once put it into practice by going to the man we had rescued and offering him all the assistance I could.

Our Guide, who had missed nothing of all this, now suggested we should take our fellow travellers to a Home or Resting House where they would be cared for and enquiries instigated to find the friends they sought. He then went forward at a brisk pace and we followed him.

It did not appear to me that we had proceeded very far when I saw a large residential house in front of us, from whose door a light was shining. I looked up into the sky, but it was quite bright, and I mused over the fact that if such a light was showing out from the house it must be a very strong one to show up so well against the light of the day.

A thought came to me, and at once the whole matter was clear. This was the house to which we were going and the light was similar to the one we had recently been given to guide us. It was now shining for the same purpose, so that we should not mistake our way.

We were greeted at the door by a man of middle age, who was delighted to give us welcome. He hurried towards us and assisted the man and woman inside. They now appeared to be nearly collapsing with fatigue. (It was later explained to me that they were affected by their transition, and needed rest to recover).

Our Guide was evidently well-known here for the inmates crowded round him when he entered, exchanging words of greeting that clearly proved that he had on many other occasions resided in that house.

He introduced Mary and myself to the Head of this establishment in a few well-chosen and kindly words. It was evident that what he said was received with approbation, for the man who had greeted us warmly commented on the fact that we were to be employed on this worthy task. He told me that many persons were brought to this Rest house, as he termed it, to recuperate until they were strong enough to continue their journey. He added that there was no real need for this, if they but knew it, but those who were unaware of the continuation of life, frequently considered that rest was necessary to them. This being fully understood, their wishes were granted to avoid any shock or hindrance to their further progress.

To those who knew or had studied this question of life after so-called death, their reception was slightly different, for they could travel forward without difficulty, and were not tired even if they had passed after some exhausting illness. Later they would rest, but only for the purpose of quickly restoring their vitality, not for the reason of resting and await their friend's arrival. From this I presumed he meant those whose religion had taught them to expect miraculous awakenings and receptions passing over Jordan.

He offered to show me over the house, for, as he stated, it will be well for you to know all about us and our work, seeing that very soon if you do the service of God in giving assistance and relief to those who require it, you will be a frequent visitor here. I accepted his offer with promptness; but before doing so I asked him why it was that I myself had no recollection of resting after passing over.

He smiled as he answered, "You already had some small knowledge of this life, for did you not enter into disputes with your friends about it? Although you did not believe in it, you were thus not so ignorant as some. Moreover you were lying on your sick bed in an unconscious condition for periods of time during which your spiritual body rested. It knew you were going to leave the physical life, for it had been told so and welcomed the order. This new body and mind of yours were all eagerness for the change to take place, so when opportunity presented itself, it rested and came over here to recuperate, leaving the physical body on the sick bed.

"You see this spiritual body had been cooped up and cramped within your physical one through your lack of interest in its growth, so on arrival here there was no further need for rest or recuperation as it is with those who have just arrived without any sort of knowledge".

"It is it possible then," I cried, "for my soul to know of my approaching demise before it occurs, and yet be unable to give that information to me?"

"Yes, that is quite possible", he answered. "Furthermore when it learns this, it proceeds in many cases to ascertain the condition and position of its next home. You failed to remember, that because your earthly garment had been discarded it does not mean that all your recollections, memories and feelings are also cast off with it. No. You are still as you were when completing your span on earth, except for having now a new covering for your soul which is the real you. That real 'you' has known many things which it has been unable to communicate to your outer self, so that the fact that it knew the time of your arrival here is not very surprising".

37
The New House

The Master of the House, for so I will term him, then conducted me to the first room that was used to receive visitors. That was a large, open room, giving outside views that were wonderful in their beauty and at the same time were very soothing. I saw flowers, trees, and grass, an expanse reaching out to some small hills in the distance. There was nothing to be seen except the beauties of nature; no houses to obstruct the view. The interior of this room was furnished for complete comfort; chairs and couches seemed to invite you to rest on them for ease.

A very happy-looking lady acknowledged our entry, and I was told that it was her special charge to receive those who came and make them welcome. She now extended that same smiling welcome to me, and at the same time offered me some fruit. I selected what to my eyes appeared to be a large plum, but if it was, then I was tasting one of the most delicious of its kind that I had even eaten. It had the same rich and ripe colour as those I had known in my past life, but its taste defied all description.

It satisfied and refreshed me as though I had partaken of some exhilarating drug but without any of a drug's bad effect.

On seeing my surprised delight, I was told that the fruit had been grown in their own gardens by one, who in the material world had specialised in their culture, and now continues his great interest. Under his present conditions this gardener was able to produce even more perfect specimens of the plum variety than the one I had just tasted.

The sole object in growing them was to provide sustenance and refreshment for tired and weary wanderers. There were also other varieties of fruit, all equally good to the eye and the palate. At a later period I tried many and can vouch for the flavour and enjoyment ascribed to them.

At the time of our visit no other person was in the room. When I commented on this fact I was told that very shortly they were expecting a number to arrive who would need attention.

On looking towards the opposite side of the room I saw a small door with a window above it. Placed in front of this window was a very large and lovely basket of flowers from which emerged a strong, bright light which poured out through the window but did not penetrate the room in which we stood.

The Master, noticing my interested stare, stated that the flowers were giving out their light to guide and help any of those travelling in the Grey Lands and enable them to reach this Home of Rest. He explained that all the thoughts of the inmates of this Home were concentrated on these flowers, and that those of higher wisdom and power also joined in their petition that this light should be constantly showing, so that those unhappy lost ones could see their way to this house and receive a ready welcome.

Sometimes, he added, those who were endeavouring to lift themselves out of their greyness were actually pursued by the evil-minded to the very gates of the Home, and in that case the light was readily accepted.

Why is it, I pondered, that the majority of men in their wretchedness and misery are never desirous of seeing one of their number escape, and endeavour to frustrate any move on the part of their fellows to obtain release? Does it give them relief to know that others are as badly off as themselves, or is it envy that makes them try to prevent others in attaining that which they, themselves are not yet ready to accept?

The answer must lie in the future of mankind. When all are able and willing to assist and help others without envy or jealousy, then the world will indeed be reaching out for spiritual advancement. Even here, the same characteristics were being exhibited as was seen by me so many times when I was in the material world, and I must honestly confess that I was equally guilty, in my way, as any of those of whom I am speaking.

My companions had stood silent as they waited for my musings to be completed. I knew that they were acquainted with the thoughts running through my mind.

On noticing my re-animation, we left the spot where the light was still steadily shining outward, and entered another room by way of a short corridor. There we found Mary with the woman she had escorted. She smiled at us as we entered, then whispering, asked us to be as quiet as possible as her charge had just fallen asleep and she considered it inadvisable to awaken her.

Our escort only smiled, then speaking in his usual kindly tone said, "it is quite all right, she will not waken for some time whatever noise is occasioned. She is gaining strength after her journey, and until her friends who have been notified arrive no efforts will awaken her. Therefore, if you wish you can leave her in the care of those who are ready to attend to her, and come with us on our tour of inspection. It will be of interest and educational value to you".

38
The Matron

Without pausing for a reply, he commenced to walk towards the further end of the room, and opening a door, stood aside to allow us to pass through.

Closing it after us, he preceded us through another lighted and ventilated corridor to another door which was opened at his approach by a lady who appeared by her dress to be a Matron or Sister. After giving us a quick scrutiny, she smiled at all of us as we passed into a very long room with a number of couches arranged round it. These were occupied by men who seemed to be recovering from some illnesses, although some of them were lying motionless.

The whole room had been tastefully decorated with flowers, and the coverings of the couches, though subdued in colour, were very harmonious. The walls looked to have been painted in some warm, golden tones, that seemed to give off their own solace and comfort. The windows, of which there were many, pervaded the whole room with a beautiful shade of blue.

Everything in the place was designed to promote rest, relaxation, and comfort.

The Matron asked if we had ever been in any of the Rest Rooms before, and on its being explained that this was our first visit, she was eager to define its purpose. She pointed out that so many people were ignorant of the continuation of life, so that when they came over here from beds of sickness, they still thought they were suffering from their old complaints. Some were unaware of their transition, and asked for the attention of nurses and others such as they had been in the habit of receiving. To avoid any shock, those who were in attendance on these people still wore the well-known dress of the Nursing fraternity. They attended to their patients in a manner similar to the Nurses of the material world, but at the same time they gave carefully guarded advice to those in their charge about the change in their condition. The main thing with which they had to contend was the ingrained ideas of some of these patients that they were suffering from diseases from which they could never recover. In one sense, physically, I suppose this is true, but in another way it is impossible, for all their diseases have been left with their discarded bodies.

Then again, some have a faint realisation of having crossed the dividing line, but have a fixed idea that they have to await the arrival of someone from Heaven to call for them. Some others, knowing that they had lost limbs before passing, cannot accept the assurance that their limbs are now whole and can be used in the normal way. It appeared that there was a medley of ideas on the whole subject that had to be eradicated before any progress could be made.

It was very evident that those who were in charge and had contact with these people, needed minds of keen perception and a deep sympathy to be able to instil confidence into persons with such deep-rooted prejudices.

A man, who previous to his transition had been a Doctor and had had great experience of mental troubles, was normally in charge of all these cases. Thus he has been carrying on the work in which he was greatly interested and eminent, ever since he arrived here. He and his little band of assistants rouse these people out of their mistaken thoughts, and send them out so that they may be with their friends and to live in the homes provided for them.

It is not always possible, however, to arouse everyone, and after great efforts have been made without avail, they are taken to what is known as the Sleeping Room where they stay until they are able to realise the foolishness of their waiting. I was assured that there are people who have been in this plight for many hundreds of Earth years. They may awake at intervals, but if they fail to see the expected visitor, or receive no summons to awake in their own preconceived manner, promptly subside into coma again. These cases are the despair of the staff and their relations, and no assistance can be given in such circumstances.

I asked why shouldn't these obstinate cases be forcibly roused to the realisation of their position. It was then gently pointed out to me that none could justly interfere with the will of anyone without infringing the law of God. He has given free will to every individual and so through their own experience they must find their own way of using it rightly. Also it is well to remember that 'Time' is nothing over here; it is only what is accomplished that is of importance.

It became perfectly obvious to me, that the mistaken teaching of the world bore strange and bitter fruits in the Spirit spheres. The ones who are the most welcome here are the people who have a knowledge, however slight, of the continuation of life; for in their cases, after a short rest, they can continue on their journey with their friends who come to meet them.

The longer I have been here, the more it has impressed itself upon me that if only men would be willing to gain a little information of the place to which they must go after so-called Death, how much happier it would be for all. At present, perhaps only one in some four thousand have this knowledge. I have been present many times when that one arrives, knowing the truth. It is indeed a pleasing sight to see him or her being met and welcomed. Their eyes are open and they have the buoyancy of youth, even in cases where they have passed to this life, full of years.

As soon as the first greetings have been given and returned, they pass along, happy and joyful, to their homes, recounting their experiences since the departure from earth of one or the other. Here there is no sign of despair, neither is there of disease, but only the glad feeling of returning Home after an absence which had to be endured.

I know this is a digression, but I am now earnestly endeavouring to force home this truth to the minds of those whom I hope will read these words.

39
The Comforting Homes

As will be noticed from the foregoing account of these Homes, everything is prepared in a very matter-off-fact way for the reception of newcomers. This was emphasised as I was shown other rooms all fully equipped and staffed ready to receive those who came. It did not matter if they already had the knowledge that they had survived 'extinction' or not; the same loving care and solitude was bestowed on all. Every possible care was taken of them and they were revigorated; then as soon as they were fit for further travel, they were given over to the care of their friends who were waiting for them.

When this truth emerges it does not appear to be very remarkable that this Home, similar to many others in these spheres, was there solely to give lonely and bewildered strangers a place in which to rest, nor is it surprising that it should be something in accordance with their own preconceived ideas of what such a Home should be. It must be remembered that most of the people who frequented these homes were still suffering from the material shock of their passing from the Earth, or of escaping from some darker planes. Therefore anything in the nature of a further shock would be additionally injurious to them. This is the reason why these Homes are planned to be like those of the material world, and all the guests treated like patients.

This fact should force those who maintain that the spirit world is unacquainted with the needs of the material world, to re-adjust their ideas in this matter, for it certainly proves that the former is very well in touch with the needs and requirements of the latter. This truth and others like it, I proved over and over again during my travels.

It would only be wearisome if I continued to describe the various rooms I entered, so I will content myself by saying that all was prepared to comfort those who entered. There was always a steady flow of people needing attention, but I was informed that sometimes when the Earth was in a turmoil, so many arrived that additional Homes were erected to cope with the rush.

I knew that I should require information as to who were the Organisers of all this, so I seized the opportunity to ask this question of the Master of the Home.

He explained that the whole of the plane in which we were now situated was divided into sections. Each section was controlled by One who came from a higher plane of activity. This personage had himself passed through the different dividing lines, and so was experienced in all their difficulties.

These difficulties he must have overcome gloriously, otherwise he would not be allowed in his present sphere. The fact that it was needful for him to give of his wisdom - obtained through experience - to others, was laid before him. No pressure is ever brought to bear to cause anyone to accept unless they are prepared to do so. On receiving his consent, he is then conducted to his particular section, which may comprise a very large expanse. It is then for him to administer it for the benefit and use of those therein, including his own co-workers. The latter, for their part, must assist all those in their community to their utmost.

The wise friend who is virtually in charge of the section, is ready and willing to give of his knowledge so that those in his care may be benefited. To assist him at all times he is in full contact with the sphere to which he really belongs. If it is necessary for him to receive any advice or assistance, it can be instantly given. For this sphere is constantly contacting the one higher, until the links of this system reach far beyond my present powers of comprehension.

The same contact is established to lower planes, of which the world is one. Thus you have a feeble description of how man is linked to God. From this it is obvious that anything that is desirable to help the enlightenment or upliftment of incarnate or discarnate spirits is readily available.

The most experienced spirit who was willing and capable, was the director of each plane of existence. Through this system the love and wisdom of God flows freely until, in a modified form it reaches the Earth. The precise fashion in which it is given is always suitable to the plane that requires it. As of course, the manner in which those planes nearer to God accept it, would not be acceptable to those lower down.

To repeat; things are tempered to suit the conditions and evolution of the occupants of the different planes of existence. From this it should be realised that the material world receives the messages and advice and help in a way that is most suited to their present mode of living. Any other way would be outside of their intelligence, and so not understandable. When the world reaches forth, ready for more knowledge, it is given, and not before. This and many more things were explained to me during my inspection of this Home.

I left my kind host with a greater understanding of the excellent organisation provided to assist our steps as we continue to progress through life. It was clear, that if we so desire, there is not a space of time in which we are not able to receive this help. Yet alas, how few times we avail ourselves of this, being more content to fritter ourselves away on minor distractions, leaving more earnest matters to settle themselves in some haphazard and mischievous way.

On my leaving the Home I said goodbye to Mary, as it was told me that she was to stay and continue her work there. Our Guide who had hitherto escorted us, also bade me farewell for the time; it having been determined that I was now capable of carrying on my work alone.

I must admit, however, that as I walked away from them, I experienced a feeling of regret that the pleasant company was no longer with me. This feeling had no sooner entered my mind, when a shaft of light appeared and touched me. By this time I had learnt that it meant that someone was desirous of giving me a message. I therefore concentrated on the light, and a voice said, "My son, you are not going out on your journey alone. The friends you have so recently left can be approached and spoken to in a similar way to this I am now using; further, those friends of yours with which you are not yet well acquainted, are very near and can be reached at all times. Whenever you are in distress or in urgent need, concentrate your mind on them and they will answer you, either to give comfort or strength. God never allows anyone who is attempting to help others, to be lonely or without friends. They may not always be seen, but they are there to give aid if it is required. Ponder on my words and you will be heartened for your work".

The voice ceased and the light faded, or so it appeared to my eyes, but inside me a greater light had been lit. Now I knew that in some slight degree I had made myself worthy of going forth to help others find their way home.

40
Continuing my Work

To recount the histories of the numbers of travellers I met and encouraged to go to the Homes, or to speak of all the opposition I had to encounter, would be tedious. So I will content myself by saying that with slight variations they were very similar to the cases of which I have already spoken when I first started out on my own travels. By some I was received as a friend, but by others I was cursed as something very evil. Yet at all times whenever I was in any difficulties, in request to my appeal for advice or assistance it was always forthcoming, as had been promised.

I was employed in this particular work for a long space, and also met many others who were engaged in a like capacity. It should be remembered that as I was writing of my own experiences, those others I met are not being introduced into my history in order to avoid complications, it is only when necessary for the lucidity of these writings that they will be presented.

I had been to one of the Homes with some newcomers, and was on the point of leaving, when a message was received asking if I could wait to greet an old friend.

I eagerly agreed and stood in the gardens surrounding the Home as I waited. It seemed that I had hardly given assent when Harold, the friend who had first received and guided me, stood by my side.

He gave me a hearty salutation which I returned with great warmth. Then after a friendly catechism from him concerning the work I had done, he said, "I suppose you are anxious to know the object of my visit?" Then seeing the intense eagerness in my face he continued, "Are you now ready to do further work for the assistance of all of those in this plane, and of many in the material form? If so I can obtain your entry into a College where you will be able to study and prepare yourself."

"On many occasions you have asked within yourself if it would be possible for you to return to the Earth to speak of your present life and past experiences. These thoughts of yours which have been seen and heard are the reason for my calling on you. To be able to act as a messenger to Earth, strict preparation is needed, for to be able to speak with any authority you must not only be taught, but shown, the whole condition of the planes nearest the Earth. Are you willing to undergo the extensive training that is necessary? Fear not to say nay if you feel you are not quite ready, and this offer will then be repeated at a later time".

I had to put restraint on myself to prevent breaking in on his speech, but now my eagerness overbore me, and I shouted out that I was willing to undertake all that he asked if only it afforded me the opportunity to carry out my secret wishes.

He smiled at my impetuosity, and clasping me by the arm said, "Come with me then, and we will see those who will be your mentors and guides in these new studies".

Then seemingly with no effort on our parts, we left the garden where we had been talking and at once stood outside the gates of what appeared to be a medieval Abbey.

Interim

The next part to be given will be the second period of history. It is therefore imperative that the writing should be so divided as to enable this to be seen clearly. It is not my intention to give this part in the same manner as the previous, for my experience of the new life by this time has given me Knowledge that is deeper and broader in its outlook.

To make sure these facts are comprehended, many arguments and questionings will be omitted. It will be shown that I obtained this wisdom by what I have done, therefore to be garrulous would destroy interest. Any explanation considered necessary will most certainly be inserted, but only new ones will be considered in this category.

As an example, I can now travel without walking in the accepted normal way. It would of course be incumbent on me to explain how I attained the Knowledge to do this. This, and other apparently mysterious actions will qualify for explanation at the proper period and in sequence. The individual aspect of my story will be retained as hitherto, so as not to confuse the reader by having too many puppets on the stage at the same time.

The whole way through the first part, it has been my ambition in these writings to place before you the real purpose of my return. That is to point out that for everyone there is a place, a condition they have already prepared for themselves by their own actions during their earth sojourn, and it is their duty to better those conditions.

Nothing stagnates, everything goes on. Thus it is with us and also with all of you.

I am only one among so many who have been allowed to give these tidings, but not all have been granted the privilege of having them recorded. This was given to me in order that I might be able in a prosaic manner to inform those still inhabiting the world I left, that another life experience goes on. My experience is not an exception, it is the Rule.

Part II

41
Arrival at College

I was now about to enter the second stage of my progression since attaining this life. This began as I entered the Abbey, for it was within that building that I was given the necessary instruction on how to pursue my studies in preparation for my future course of work.

Upon entering, I was conducted through the halls to a beautifully carved and scrolled door. This was open and I was courteously invited to enter. The interior of this room was panelled in oak, with tables and seats of the same material. On the centre table was a light that came from a beautiful bowl, giving out diffused beams to illuminate the room. This light harmonised with the whole room, making it restful and conducive to relaxation and thought.

I did not have very long to examine it then, but at a later period I frequented it on many occasions, and it bore out my first impressions.

A side door opened and a man came up to me saying, "I am very pleased to give you greeting on your arrival here. I have been accorded the privilege of being your instructor for a time. Your earnest desire to acquaint yourself with the knowledge of your present condition has been passed to me, so therefore it is incumbent on me to assist you by all manner of means. You must not, because of that, consider that I am in any way your superior, but simply that I have had a little more experience, and through that experience I can help you to accomplish your mission".

He paused and I took the opportunity to thank him for his kindness and generous offer.

He then continued, "You will remain here as long as it is considered necessary, so that you become acquainted with certain processes we have in contacting the different planes, of which the Earth is one. You will be quite free to move about and pay visits, but it is requested of you that you will give the greater portion of your time to your studies. This should not prove irksome if you really desire to accomplish your ambition.

I hastily broke in to assure him that I would willingly co-operate to the best of my ability.

He smiled at my eagerness and added," I have no doubt of that, but it is as well to be informed of what is required at the beginning, as it saves tedious explanations later. Your course of studies embraces the attaining of the laws that operate here. Without the knowledge of these laws your task would be a failure."

"The whole idea is to prime you with the conditions of this life, so that when you are able to return to Earth you will be in a position to describe them faithfully and accurately to those with whom you speak. It will all be shown to you, so that you will be able to acquire the requisite knowledge. We do not allow those who are unacquainted with these truths to return to their former life, and pose as being in a position to give the facts. Much harm would be done that way. Unfortunately that is a favourite trick of those of low evolution to do this, but if the right questions are asked of them, they are very quickly discomposed and hastily retreat.

"You must be in a position to answer relevant questions honestly, and with one purpose only - that is to give to the Earth children the truth. During the course of your late work it must have forcibly been brought to your notice how few arrive here with any intelligent understanding of where they have landed. It will be part of your duty to try to ensure that more will know where they are to stay after leaving the earth."

"This is no mean task, as you will find when it is time for you to commence. By some you will be welcomed, by others condemned, and many will be entirely indifferent to your approaches. You will have to bear all this with equanimity combined with considerable patience. Yet as this is God's work, it cannot fall, so let that give you the needed comfort to do it with a joyous zest".

After a pause he then continued, "Let me first introduce you to your fellow students, then after you have meditated and rested, I will come to you again and we will make a beginning".

He turned, and followed by me, went out through the door by which he had entered. We crossed through a long corridor and entered a large Hall.

42
Profound Preparation

I very quickly ascertained that what I may term my 'fellow students were very conscientious in their studies. They certainly gave me a hearty welcome, but after a brief interlude with them I was well aware of their intentness and perseverance.

In this plane where we were now it was impossible to hide one's feelings, thoughts, or emotions. It should be appreciated that there was no physical body behind which one could hide or cower. Our thoughts and feelings were in a sense naked. What we felt and thought appeared clearly; it was to be seen and read by anyone who wished to obtain a knowledge of our aspirations. Deceit could not be practised in any shape or form, your character and worth was fully exposed. If I had not been considered worthy of perusal by my fellows, I know I should not have been allowed to enter here, so this thought encouraged me.

This fact is well worth considering by those of you who will one day arrive here in these realms. Therefore it is better for you to so order your inner life that the need for pretence is not needed. In this way a great strain will be taken from you.

Consider a man, who, during the whole of his life has been a hypocrite, posing from outward appearances as a kind and benevolent person. Yet inwardly his thoughts have been darkened by mean, unjust, or filthy contemplations. He arrives after a time on this plane of existence, and, unconscious of the loss of his material body, endeavours to pose as he did formerly. His words may be of a kindly nature, yet even as he is speaking, his thoughts which now speak louder than his voice, betray him to those with whom he is in contact. This is an example of which I have seen many, and how disgusting and grotesque they are! There is common sense in cleaning the mind as well as the body; if you will but do it, you will avoid being such a spectacle.

Many of those with whom I was now associating were undertaking this intensive study for the purpose of teaching on the earth plane, but a goodly number were destined to do the same on the spirit plane. Yes, even here teaching is always necessary in one way or another, even though you have left the physical world. So many have need of it, for, alas, so many have arrived here uneducated as far as their future interests are concerned. They may have lived pure and unselfish lives and yet lack the knowledge of the uses of immortality. Therefore teachers are made available to supply this want in their progression.

I do not intend to give all the details about the period I passed in the Abbey, but I will summarise the course I passed through. The initial stages were those of preparation. It was apparent from these that everything possible is done to make us acquainted with our own natures. Our antecedent history was perused to find out the lessons we had learned and also those in which we had failed or overlooked. These, especially the latter were subjected to a strict but not unkindly scrutiny, until a thorough understanding of the motives, influences, and other extraneous matters were seen in the proper perspective. Nothing was too small or too large to be overlooked. The defects in my own mind and character were focused, so that I should be well aware of the need to watch myself very carefully when any idea or action should bring them in touch with the acts that had caused my downfall. The good points were emphasised so that they might be improved at the proper period. My spiritual short-sightedness was shown to me time and time again so that I might become mentally alert at all times. Then after this had been accomplished and I had seen and understood for myself my various needs, a picture of what I might have been whilst on earth was built up. This was to show me what I could have made of my life if I had had the knowledge or had endeavoured to obtain it.

This picture was not, what my earth friends might have imagined it to be one of normally conventional existence, as they had conceived my life to be. On the contrary it showed me failing, faltering, and stumbling, for like a child I had been weak and needed help and teaching. Yet after a while in this picture I seemed to gain strength, and avoided many pitfalls. But there were still some I could not avoid, for the experience of them had been needed by my spiritual self, and so I had had to ensure and fall in order to emerge from them triumphantly.

It was pointed out that it was impossible to be perfect whilst on Earth, for the spirit is not then ready for perfection; by this I mean perfection in the sense attributed to those near to God. It is only the pains, trials and tribulations that help to perfect the spirit, in the same way as the joys and gladnesses perform a like thing by illuminating and giving power to it. The consolidation of all this creates a soul desirous of approaching God, but, knowing at the same time its imperfections, it is quite willing to wait and be taught these things necessary for such a glorious meeting.

That was how I saw matters after the pictures and lectures had been given me.

43
Fundamental Truths

Is it strange that use should be made of our Earth experiences to gain an insight as to the potentiality of that future life? I think not. For underlying all the reasons for having to pass a span of time physically, there is the reason that without such preparation nothing progressive can be accomplished.

This is the fundamental condition that you should become acquainted with, your spiritual strengths and weaknesses, and from them gain power and wisdom to overcome them or to encourage your spirit.

I did not, of course, absorb this reasoning quickly. It was only obtained after an accumulation of ideas and thoughts had been digested. Yes, that is the purpose of your life on Earth, both now and for a very long time indeed. There is nothing given carelessly. Whatever you receive, you have earned it. Rewards or punishments are all just, for you gain them in due proportion according to your deserts. This is the unalterable law of God.

My Teachers were all men or women - for we had many of the latter - who had, themselves, experienced all the joys and pitfalls of approaching the physical world and forming contacts. They knew of the suspicions and ignorance prevailing; they were also very appreciative of the joys in uniting with those who were desirous of these friendships.

They spoke continually of their gladness in returning to their physical friends, and of the welcome given them. This, they affirmed out weighed all the other ills. Many were sincerely attached to the instruments or persons they used for the purpose of teaching the continuity of life. These experienced Spirits lectured us on the means to be used to obtain suitable conditions under which to work. They further gave us illustrations of the manner in which ill-conditioned, frivolous, and spiteful Spirits would endeavour to interfere with us as we descended to Earth conditions; whilst we were there; and on our return journey.

It was fully explained to us the necessity of taking with us those who were strong enough to afford protection against such as were determined to hinder our work and harm us. Under no circumstances were we to allow the slightest obstruction to be persisted in. It was strongly pointed out that there were so many spirits of poor development or progressiveness who would try to thwart anything we were doing, and if they were allowed to succeed in their attempts they were heartened thereby, and would quickly do much worse than merely obstruct.

We, our Teachers told us, would never be alone, but it was always necessary for us to understand that those who assisted us could not shoulder our responsibilities for us. Whatever we said or accomplished was entirely ours and no other could accept it.

All this and very much more did I learn during this first period of my instruction. I now began to notice that my memory which used to be so vagrant, was becoming so capable that once

I had learned anything, it was retained, and produced whatever was needed when it was required. As it was no longer clogged by physical clothing it functioned perfectly.

Thus, when I first saw the history of my life, it was memory that provided the details in all their meanings. So it was now, when the demand was made, that memory gave forth its accumulation of wisdom. If I gave out faint impressions, the reason was not far to seek; the lesson had not been thoroughly learnt, and you therefore went over it again. Your memory always has, and will always be, with you as far as I can ascertain; so keep it active, stored with good things, and then there will be less to regret later on.

After I had satisfactorily passed through this part of my tuition, I was taken on a tour of other planes of existence. I was as yet unable to accomplish this through my own strength, but our Teachers added their own power, and we were able to travel in comparative ease.

When I speak of 'travelling', it must be appreciated that this movement is entirely different to the manner I had adopted on Earth. We only use that form of travel for amusement or to revive old memories. Now we moved by the power of concentration and in a full belief that what we wanted - if it was unharmful - would be granted.

Thus, should we desire to go to a distant plane, we concentrated on it and asked permission to go there and be hospitably received. Then, those in the plane we wished to visit - if they approved, and I never knew one that did not give us welcome - poured thought-strength towards us and we were thus enabled to be there.

If we so desired, we could travel in a leisurely manner, viewing the scenery and places as we passed through. If we decided to hasten, we were there as soon as the thought had fastened itself in our minds. This mode has always given me the impression that we did not move but that the plane we were visiting came to **us**. This so far is true for that plane is always there, but we break through the intervening power or rays that had hid it from our sight.

It is very hard to explain, but if you can imagine being lost in a mist, and thinking you are in one place, then, suddenly the fog lifts and you see you are in another place of which you had thought but decided was impossible to reach. This is the nearest I can get to explain the manner of our fast travel. So I fear I must leave it there.

44
Difficulties of Communicating with the Physical Plane

It should be borne in mind that all the teaching given here is for a very definite purpose. It is to ensure success in our undertakings, and to obtain the confidence of those of you to whom we speak.

It is quite possible, even here, that some persons have not quite the requisite qualities for this mutual gift of getting and retaining the loyalty and confidence of those we contact in the physical. Because we have arrived here it does not mean that we have overcome our diffidence at speaking and convincing strangers. We may perhaps, be able to receive encouragement and wisdom more easily, perhaps, but when the necessity arises for us to give it out, then it is that our personality comes into question.

If you were able to see the other side when a Séance is being held, you would very easily understand my meaning. To begin with, there are those who throng round, waiting a chance to destroy or paralyse our efforts, and they have first to be overcome. Then there is the unfortunate fact, which cannot be avoided, that we are clothed in what might be termed a protective armour; for we cannot come to you in our usual condition as we are here. If we did, it would either cause injury to the Medium, or we should be so badly buffeted by your heavy and foggy conditions as to be incapable of any effort. Then, even when so guarded and protected, it needs great perseverance and strength to penetrate and get our message through to you.

Again, in transmission, whatever we give is liable to distortion or suppression. Sometimes I have wondered if we are not very fortunate if we manage to get anything through to you at all, for those of you who **should** assist us are often content to rest on your laurels and give out nothing. But those who are actively inclined against us, and our purpose, are **always** in evidence.

From all the foregoing you can see that it is very evident that instruction and guidance in our work is extremely necessary.

My recreation, during the course of my studies, was obtained by visiting many parts of the land of which I was now an inhabitant. By this means I was able to obtain first-hand knowledge of the many things I ought to know, and so be able to answer questions. During this period I made many friends and met mutual acquaintances, and was thus able to keep up with the interests of both worlds.

After what appeared to be a long period, I was informed by the Head of the Abbey that I had now received sufficient teaching to go on elsewhere, and put some of it into practice. I was not to consider that I was ready yet to undertake my hoped for mission to Earth, but I was to be taken in hand by one who was capable of giving me knowledge of more practical things by showing me the various organisations and planes of my present realm. I was to be conducted, with a few others who had been chosen as my companions, over the surrounding territory, and introduced to those best suited to prepare me for my future work.

It was with a feeling of deep regret that I finally said goodbye to my teachers and fellow students, although by now I was well acquainted with the mode of speaking and being with them again in a space of time no longer than a flash of light. Yet I still felt the separation; for all of them, unfailingly, had endeavoured to do everything in their power to help me. Their constant kindness and courtesy has been one of the greatest things I have carried away with me, and is an everlasting bright memory still.

It was not long before I was told that my new Instructor had arrived and awaited my convenience. He appeared to be of a different nationality to myself, and for a time I was unable to satisfy myself as from what nation he had originally come. Later I discovered that he was an Egyptian by birth, but that his Mother had been a Caucasian. He had been in these realms for a very long time, and owing to his constant travels, he had assimilated many traits of the peoples and places he had visited, so that he was very cosmopolitan.

I shall not worry you with his description, but content myself by remarking that he was an admirable guide and friend. He was able to take us all, without any mishaps, on the explorations we needed. He was met and treated with respect by all those with whom we came in contact. He resided on a different plane to that we were now inhabiting, as he had progressed from our plane a long space back! But he was always content to give of his knowledge and advice when required.

But because of this, it must not be assumed that he evinced any signs of superiority; the reverse was the case. Our Conductor was most companionable and of very even temperament. During the whole of the period I was with him, or in his charge, I never noticed him disturbed. He was an example of toleration and understanding that was of great benefit to me.

The first part of our journey was to explore the country in which we resided. It was an illuminating tour, for although I had travelled through it before, I had not really examined it closely. Under guidance many interests were discovered. I had not previously thoroughly mastered the idea of activity in the way in which I now saw it. To give some idea of what I mean I will endeavour to portray a very little of what was shown to me.

With the others I went to a town quite near, and was shown over what might be described as a business premises. The Manager of this place was a man who on Earth was well known for his ability to organise and make a success of this kind of venture. This had been his greatest interest and, as he had at the same time assisted and helped others, he was allowed for a space to do the same work here.

There are many others who have a great interest in this kind of work here, and so they joined the business. Now here is where the difference between a business on Earth and over here, entered.

In the world the gain was taken by those immediately concerned. A recognised thing and no wrong action if it has been accomplished justly. But here that principle has been changed. The whole business is run for the benefit of all, for to endeavour to reward anyone financially over here is unthought of and perfectly useless. So this business supplied the wants of the townspeople to the best of its ability, and asked in return that they should be recompensed in the only way suitable; that is to say by a service in which they were not skilled.

Thus we will say, the Manager, owing to his work in the business was unable to find time to keep house, so will have those needs done for him by persons able to do such service. Then again, those who are able to build houses may be incapable of caring for an orchard. They in their turn, in return for their work, can call in those who are skilled in fruit-farming. This is how all things are carried out here. Everything is for the community and nothing for self.

On the planes of lower evolution things are of course different. The one of which I am speaking now was a progressive plane. On enquiry I was told that there was never any reluctance on the part of the inhabitants to obey this code of ethics. If they had they could not have been here, for such a defect would have barred their entry.

I saw the social side of this plane very intimately, for we were all invited to stay at any of the houses on which we called, and there were many we entered. We were entertained, and opinions asked and given on every possible subject. Yes, even on our impressions of the World we had left, and of our present one. I was interested to note that there was often a divulgence of views on the subject of the future uses of our present life.

45

The Prevalence of Differences of Opinions

It is most necessary for you to know that differences of opinions and views on various matters is very prevalent on this plane, but there is not the animosity usually exhibited by those who hold strong beliefs. It is well known here that none of us are capable of grasping the whole of the potentialities of this new world in which we are, and thus we are really eager to have our views influenced by any who are able to do this. There is a concord of opinion that God is the creator of all the Worlds and everything therein, and that He is beyond and above any suspicion of corruption, and therefore until we can be the same, we shall never reach Him. We believe that Jesus has already charted the way so that we can follow the course that He has marked and eventually reach Him.

How and when this is to be done was the subject of many of the conversations I had with those with whom I was now frequenting.

I also found that the "payment", if it can be so described, by service was universal here. But I was quickly informed that this did not apply to other planes lower than this one. The people here were contented and happy, and some were preparing to go to higher or broader planes of existence.

There were many who questioned our Conductor unceasingly for his description and ideas on those planes he had visited. Many of these enquirers had already been taken to their new homes on a temporary visit, but that had only made them more eager for further knowledge about them.

When these fortunate ones leave, they will not lose touch with their present friends for, as I have explained elsewhere, they can communicate with one another in a flash. Also those who go higher can always descend for a short period, although those lower cannot ascend without help from the higher.

During our tour I visited many Churches but found those here differed entirely from those I had previously known. The teaching now given was the same which Christ gave when he was in the physical world. The old trappings and discrepancies had been jettisoned, for now they were able to obtain His exact statements, for all those are stored here; the whole of His life, truthfully shown can be seen by the earnest Enquirer.

What a revelation that must be to the hide-bound orthodox person! I have seen this record and the Earth version is hardly recognisable beside it. I now really understood how He became the Saviour of mankind; a thing I had never been able to do before. Those persons who were incapable of recognising this, or were so prejudiced that they would not accept it are not here. They have their own plane where they can congregate and worship in their own old manner until they are prepared to accept the truth.

The Persons I spoke to, were, nearly all, men who had preached and taught to the best of their ability the truth, as they saw it while on Earth. They had, early in their physical life, recognised the divergences of so-called religion and had earnestly searched for the fallacies in it. Some were those who had been able to see their false position on arrival here, and had straightway thrown overboard that which they found to be untrue. All of them were now seeking to the utmost of their powers to obtain more truth about God, and had obtained it from the fountain of wisdom - Jesus Christ. Although He is still so far away, yet His presence and influence is stronger than it has ever been.

You can judge from this how invigorating and heartening it was to be able to talk to these men. They professed simply nothing in regard to their calling, but were content to say that they were only His disciples, endeavouring to give forth and practice His teachings. To my joy they were unanimous in this and there was no rivalry as to the particular way to be followed; they gave welcome, and of their best to all.

After a while I found that many had belonged to rival and antagonistic religions on Earth, but now this had all gone and they were in harmony. Indeed a case of the lions lying down with the lambs!

From them I received many shrewd words of advice to assist me in my work when it commenced, and many times since I have offered up thanks. For their words have been my mainstay in doubts and difficulties when trying to break down the incredulity and doubts of the material world.

46
Progress of Knowledge
& Understanding

The realm that we were now in was not Heaven. That place - and I deem it very far away - was a land wherein the people realised the responsibilities of their enduring life, and were prepared to adjust their natures to it in more spiritual alignment. To be able to realise this fact alone, was of great assistance in enriching the soul, for it goes on for a time indeterminate, but ultimately there will be a cessation to continued progressive aspirations. When that peak is reached, the Soul will have acquired all the wisdom from experience that it needed, and be able to rest, tranquil and contented. This is how I imagine the distant future will be for each one of us.

After exploring the house, gardens, workshops, halls and places of amusement - and there are plenty of the latter kind - we re-grouped to study the results of our experiences. Our Conductor subjected us to a torrent of questions, all given to ensure that what the whole group had experienced should be given for the benefit of all.

This really meant that we all became acquainted with everything each of us had learned; it all went into a common fund from which we received an overwhelming share. Thus, practically nothing of importance was missed. Our memories, lacking the physical, were alert and retentive to a degree that surprised me. It was now no effort on our part to remember; indeed it would have needed great strength to forget!

After each had given their version, our Conductor informed us that we were going to broader and higher realms for more teaching. We should have to have help to be able to do this, for unaided we should not be able to reach them.

As he concluded this message I saw the beam of light which always shows that a message had arrived, touch his head. He concentrated for a while and then told us that those who were going to aid us and be our hosts, were with us.

By that time I was well acquainted with the rapidity of motion, but the quickness with which these personages were in our midst astonished me. They spoke to our Leader, not in words but through thought, then turning to us, bowed slightly and merrily asked us if we were ready for the journey.

Now to describe these Personages is rather puzzling, for their different nationalities was not very apparent at first. Even now I am not sure where they came from. They conversed with us in a similar manner to which they had done with our Conductor, so there was nothing to be gleaned. If they had spoken in words a clue might have been obtained from their accents. Their costumes were tunic dresses, comfortable and durable, like those some of us were wearing. The only extra was a small jewel that flashed enchantingly from their belts. Later I found that this was the only indication that they came from a different sphere of activity. These jewels were only allowed to be worn by those who had earned the right to have them, by living a wise and well-chosen course of life. That they were persons of wide intellect could very easily be perceived; men not to be trifled with, but tolerant and understanding, with a loving knowledge of the frailties and weaknesses of less well endowed people. They appeared to be grave; but underneath this aspect there was a bubbling spring of joy and humour that was contagious. They accepted us all as welcome visitors and seemed determined to make our visit as pleasant as it was possible for them to make it.

This time we requested that instead of passing rapidly to our new destination, we might travel in a more leisurely manner so as to be able to obtain a view of anything we passed through. After a short conversation this was agreed upon.

Our hosts then requested us to group together, and one of them went to the front, the other two went on either side of us, while our Conductor kept behind. Then we all began to move slowly upward with an easy and free movement that was effortless and pleasant.

The plane in which we had been, receded beneath our feet, and looking down it appeared as if a mist had covered it so that it was hard to discern. Soon this mist became so thick that I lost sight of the plane entirely; so I turned my head upwards to try to see where we were.

47
Visiting New Spheres

It was conceivable that we were now in an atmosphere that was incapable of giving sustenance to any life whatsoever. It appeared capable of allowing us to breathe, but that was all.

I am afraid that I glanced rather disappointedly around me, which caused considerable amusement to our couriers.

Then, suddenly, as though the fog and mistiness had been wiped away by a giant hand, I saw the outline of another world.

We approached it, or it came towards us, I am never certain which, as we slowly travelled over it. There were people actively engaged in various pursuits, who waved to us. They failed to exhibit any signs of surprise or amazement at our entry or mode of travelling.

It was a very fine country, with rolling downs and small rivers that sparkled and glistened in the light. The Towns or Cities were neither thronged with crowds nor packed with houses. There were more open spaces and gardens than I have ever noticed before, and the houses exhibited better taste in their architecture and design. It was clearly apparent that beauty of design was the key-note of those who had built these towns.

The people I saw were not wearing clothing like that to which I had become accustomed. They had robes of the type of a Roman Toga, yet not quite as I had previously seen them, but this is the best description I can give. Of course there were variations of colour and design, but the whole effect was one of simplicity and beauty. They seemed to be imbued with the life of the wearer and gave forth a shimmering delight that appealed to all my senses.

Upon enquiring where we were, I was informed that this was a sphere broader and more cultured than the one we had so recently left. These inhabitants had earned the right to be there by their toleration and understanding of others, and a bigger grasp of the purity of God's wishes for His children. These people had been able to forgive sincerely and to pardon, before asking to be pardoned; to be able to give love, prior to receiving it themselves. Surely the reversal of the usual formula of ordinary life! To me, as I gazed, it seemed a wonderful place and country in which to reside.

Then a voice broke in on my thoughts and I looked round to ascertain who of my companions was speaking. I then saw that they were all silent and intently listening. The voice was coming from one of the Towns. It gave us all greeting in the name of God, and good wishes in our travels. Then it asked if we would be gracious enough to stop and visit their country on our return journey. They were acquainted with the reason why we should not tarry now, but warmly asked us to consider their request on our return.

Our Leader must have replied through concentration, for the Voice thanked us for our answer and then ceased.

My companions all burst into happy laughter and questioned our Guides as to the reason why we could not stop now and visit these unknowns ones who were so friendly disposed towards us.

But we were told that as we had further to travel, the strength and power necessary to get us to the appointed place was being conserved on our outward journey, so as to enable us to have more time there. But on the return trip this consideration would be unnecessary, and so those who wished could stay for awhile. In a way I was glad of this, for I was anxious to reach as high as it was possible for me to do.

We all proceeded slowly on our way, passing through different stratas of the sky, which to my surprise I discovered to be densely populated.

It was explained to me that I was allowed to see this through the power that was being used to take us to our destination, as I was changing with the changing vibrations. This, of course applied to all of us. It was my first practical experience of being vibratingly "built up", if this is the term that can be used to describe it, but I know of no other way to explain the change. It really seems that we are all "life" in the lighter, or rarer environment to which we are suited.

To obtain this result we have to be conditioned spiritually, so there is no need of bars to prevent our entry. We are very much, I thought, like a fish on land, gasping, and wanting to return to the place to which we are most suited.

The scenery of this plane was not only beautiful but intense. It seemed to hearten as well as beautify. Many messages of welcome were relayed to us as we passed through, and we appeared to be respected as honoured guests.

I was informed that if we were travelling in a downward direction, that is to the lower planes, that what we were experiencing would be in a reverse ratio, and we could have expected much unpleasantness.

Later I endured a travel in this direction through the Grey Lands and experienced most unpleasing feelings. These words are a gross understatement, but I am content to leave it at that; it is not nice to describe horrors.

How long we were on our journey I have no means of knowing, and the period of it passed very rapidly. Our Conductors stated that we were now approaching their own homes, and requested us to be ready to catch the first glimpse of it.

We all eagerly peered ahead, each one trying to be the first to see it. I was standing near one of our Leaders and he turned and directed my gaze towards what appeared to be a bright light. If I had not been expecting something different, I should have surmised that it was the sun just rising in the distance. But as I looked more closely I saw that there was a variety of iridescence around these lights that were swirling about, forming harmonies of colour. It may give you some conception of what I saw if I say that it looked like a large number of rainbows, but with more grades of hues, that were twisting and circling round this light. It was so overwhelming that I was very glad that our Conductors were with us.

On noticing my confusion, one of them laughingly explained that the colours were the life-giving force of the planet on which they resided, and that it was the evidence of the strength and power of God. Without it there could not be any existence there, but with it, God's presence was manifested. They welcomed and relished the thought that we were approaching this maelstrom of beauty and colour.

48
Arrival

We entered the zone of the radiance of colour very quickly, and I found that it gave me a feeling of overwhelming confidence and strength. The atmosphere entered into my being so much that I felt capable of attempting anything that might be needed: a complete contrast to my feelings a little earlier.

I now realised how a plane of existence could "live" in the sense that the whole of this one was alive. The air, the earth and the inhabitants were all really alive, and not something apart from the persons dwelling thereon.

As we neared the land, I saw a beautifully constructed Tower which stood out as if it were a beacon and refuge; a haven of safety for weary travellers. It had verandas and gardens which were thronged with people waiting to give us welcome. All these people were acutely alive as could be seen by the intensity of their smiling greetings. There was nothing half-hearted about their reception of us, and it came naturally from them. Any idea of hypocrisy was unthinkable.

They were there ready to assist us in all possible ways without a thought of reward or advantage.

Their clothing was of various hues, in the usual comfortable robe-style with sleeves, on which I have remarked before. Health and Youth in all its grandest features were there to be seen, with knowledge and wisdom on their faces. It was impossible to look at them without appreciating their superiority and our own inferiority.

They had attained what we were still striving to gain - wisdom, youth, and eternal life.

My thoughts flew back to the poor use I had made of my own life; forgetting for the moment that these thoughts could be so easily read, until the nearest of our Couriers turned to me and said in a sympathetic tone, "Yes, this is all so different to the Earth life, but you must hearten yourself with the knowledge that God allows all of us to proceed from the Earth life to a finer and better one. All these friends who are awaiting us here have experienced the common lot of us all, that of being encased in a physical body. Some of them descended lower than you have done, but through their very mistakes they eventually gained these shores, and rest here awhile before going on further.

"You must learn that there are many more spheres of life beyond this one where knowledge and joys unknown are to be found, and ultimately all will reach them. So be not sad and sorrowful over your own apparently lowly place. This is the reason you have been brought here, that when you return to your own plane this experience will strengthen you to go forward".

I sincerely thanked this friend for his comforting words, and prepared myself for the meeting, determined to acquire all the information it would be possible to obtain, and store it for future reference and reflection.

By this time we had reached the Tower which was very large and could accommodate a great number of people. There were no door-ways to give or bar entrance. It was open for every one to enter or leave at will. Somewhere, but out of my view, was an orchestra; singers were singing songs, and music reached my ears. I had no idea of their songs, but the music was evidently that of instruments that were entirely unknown to me. I should have liked to have rested and listened to it, but on being assured that I could have more of it later when desired, I now followed my companions.

There were two personages who separated themselves from the waiting crowd as we settled on the veranda of the Tower. They looked so much alike that I formed the opinion that they were related, but this was not substantiated when I heard them being introduced as distinct and separate persons. I later found that all who resided here were superficially alike, as the majority were alike in thought and temperament, although underneath they were unmistakably different.

49
New Revelations

I have given the particulars of my journey and arrival in this wider plane of life, but am unable to give in detail all I saw and studied through lack of words in which to portray it suitably.

It should be remembered that this plane has knowledge of the conditions of life that are indescribable, and it is not until you have advanced, plane by plane to a great height, that you will be capable of assimilating these things. Not that they are mysteries, but only greatly advanced learning. But it requires previous study and preparation before they can be understood. I shall therefore content myself by summarising my visit as a whole.

I was surprised to learn that there were two distinct types of people on this plane; the advanced inhabitants who had earned a right to be here and whose home it was, and "others" who were responsible for work of a more material nature.

These "others" were only interested in the natural things of life as you and I understand them, as a simple interest and relaxation. They admired scenery, hills, flowers and similar beauties, but made no effort to increase or alter them in any manner of form, and the care of it was in their hands. It was left entirely to them and they only had a slight contact with the rightful Inhabitants who frequented this plane. It was not a case of condescension, but the rightful knowledge that those who were labouring in this direction, were doing that which would ultimately increase their spiritual worth, so they were left to fulfil their impulses. Further, these more elementary spirits were encouraged to go on, but never once did I see any trespassing in their work.

They had their duty to perform, and when completed, theirs was the full reward.

The highly evolved people among whom I was, had risen above any suggestion of physical desires and appetite. There were fruit trees in abundance, but it was rarely that the fruit was picked, the trees were there for their colouring and perfume. The whole of the air seemed to be impregnated by such perfume that had never reached me before. It contained strength, vitality, and if required could create within oneself soothing repose.

The eating of anything was unknown, or if tried was for experimental purposes only. Wild animals were missing, only a few of the mild and innocent kind, such as deer, gazelles and such like remained; they were now fearless and beautiful to behold. Nor were any kept as domestic pets; all led their real existence. Birds of a variety of colours and plumage filled the air with their glad songs. They appeared to me to be a more superior type to any I had ever previously known. As they flew over head, there was such a sheen coming from them that any descriptive phrases could not do justice to its delicacy.

There were flowers, both small and large, many of species and shapes unknown to me, and all were giving of their best in the way of perfume and beauty. Everything capable of giving forth anything that would be pleasing to the eyes or the senses, was on this plane.

The houses were made of some sort of stone that would have rivalled any of the rarest or costliest marbles that were on the Earth. They were cut and assorted into colours and sizes, and built up into walls. All was so artistically done that the walls seemed to shimmer like the reflection of water with the sun on it, but a hundred times more lovely.

The houses all lacked doors, and the only bar to entrance, if such it could be called, was a cloth of many-coloured tapestry. This either hung straight down, or was drawn partly aside. Embroidered on this cloth was, usually, the occupant's name; I mean the name they now owned, and should not be confused with the usual surnames of the world. Some of these names were floral, whilst others had a meaning which had to be explained to me.

The interiors of these houses were not at all palatial. Although the furniture was rare, there was not a great deal of it. Finely wrought tapestries were there in abundance, with couches and similar resting places, but a complete absence of beds is the rule rather than the exception. As sleep is unnecessary there is no reason to make provision for it. The houses might be deemed to be places in which friends could meet to discuss any topic that was considered suitable, but not to be used in which to pass the greater part of their lives. As those persons I met seemed to be always engaged in some work that took them away from home, it was only for recreation that the houses were needed.

Many of the Inhabitants spent long spaces away on other planes, teaching, or helping others, or perhaps going further afield to obtain knowledge and wisdom for themselves. There were many who never even occupied a house at all, they were content to relax in the beautiful country around them. If they required quietness and solitude they were able to build round themselves a barrier, or different vibrations, by means of concentration and so were unseen by any who came near.

The solidarity of the whole of the grounds and buildings, also of the men, women, and children was unquestionable. There is nothing shadowy or tenuous about any of the spheres.

The principal employment of the people I met was the correct conveyance of messages and instruction to those for whom they are intended. The thoughts and prayers from Earth people are transmitted by those who are authorised to receive them on this plane, and if necessary to strengthen and clarify them before being passed to a higher authority for a decision and reply. Then, when the answer is received from higher up, it is transmitted to those whose duty it is to get it returned to the petitioner.

Not all thoughts and prayers from Earth reach here, for if they are weak or wavering, they are dealt with by others nearer to the sender. Some never require an answer for they are blotted out by the person sending them, owing to a contrary one being immediately sent to follow the first one. Selfish or thoughtless prayers hardly ever reach even as far as the plane nearest the Earth, for these are seized upon by those who batten on such things.

There are many near your world who are eager to be the recipients of such foolish petitions, and as the appetite of these lowly-evolved souls are whetted, they soon cluster round the one sending them. They will then use all of their scarce knowledge to some influence, for their purpose is to encourage even more foolish petitions to be sent out, as they recognise kindred souls.

The reverse is also applicable, for should the thoughts and prayers be unselfish and charitable, then those who can strengthen and encourage the sender gather near to assist. So it behoves everyone to guard their thoughts, for they are very real and easily read and seen by all of us who have cast off the physical body.

If I should be required to give a name to the plane I was now visiting, I should call it The Land of Wisdom. All therein had passed through various vicissitudes, and through this had gained their knowledge by experience. They were all ready at all times to help in a very practical way with their acquired wisdom. Yes, even the children were gaining their maturity through the experiences of their older companions.

The reason for this was given me by one of them, who explained that he had had only a short Earth life - a matter of minutes. But in accordance with the desire of those who were near to God and knew of His wishes, the child was taken to the children's plane, or sphere. Here he was cared for, taught the real purpose of the usefulness of life - viz. - to help and love all those he met.

After a period, as he grasped what was required, he moved further afield, passing through teacher after teacher until he had arrived in his present plane. Here with others he will be able to have a full Earth experience, for when he is ready he will go back to be near those who are living a material existence and will be among those of his own nature or group. Then he will be able to be joyous with them, or perhaps, have to stand sorrowfully aside as he sees them plunge into harm. He will feel that, and yet have to remain aloof, unable to help. Naturally the one he is watching so closely is that one who is carrying out the plan that might have been his if he had survived to have an Earth life.

50
God's Loving Care

The conception of eternal life as a long period of disused opportunities, of continuous resting and relaxation, is unknown; instead the knowledge that it must be used for a benevolent and helpful purpose is predominant.

It may be considered that whilst a physical person is very active in the use of their body, it cannot compare with the restlessness and activity of their mind. So on leaving their physical attributes behind they still have the mind, which is then free and unencumbered. It is thus easily imagined how mental activity is increased.

It is when I speak of those with whom I was now mingling as being "actively" engrossed in their work, that something of their earnestness and purpose may be learned. Their minds were so educated that by their knowledge they are capable of making, altering, or designing anything that is to their good. I have seen these persons, by concentration, cause beautiful buildings to be erected, or perhaps it is more correct to say "appear" to me as I looked. They have created scenes from the past with the original characters acting their parts in the same way as they had done when they had physical bodies.

At my request these actors have informed me where they had been wrong in their earthly parts, and shown me the corrected life as it should have been lived for that period. Everything that has occurred on the Earth plane is known and can be reproduced if, and when required. It is not a merely visionary sight, but actuality. How far back their knowledge extends I have never enquired, but there does not appear to be any limitation as far as I understood it.

The fact that they are in easy contact with those of broader and higher development, opens up the thought that it could go on in this manner until the light of the Spirit of the Universe is reached. This leads to an enlightening idea of how God can guide and control his children through His messengers. This should give rise to a new feeling of confidence in those who may have doubted the thought that God knows all the joys and sorrows of those now on this Earth.

It may now be understood why I was brought to this plane; it was to furnish me with concrete facts about a more developed life than any other I had previously known. Unless I had actually entered in to it I should never have been able to explain the love and care that God has for us all. Through this experience I am able to state that that great love is with us, for I have seen it in operation.

There are of course, other means to ensure the carrying out of His laws, but this manner of so doing attracted me a little more strongly than the others, and so gave me a better understanding.

51
Following the
Teachings of Jesus

I was unable to trace any particular forms of religion, in the sense that creeds of any kind were absent here. Yet all possessed a deeply rooted knowledge of God. It was not only how they spoke about His loving care, but their profound understanding of it that so impressed me. It was accepted with the assured conception of Him as a Father and also a friend. Everything that had happened to them was received as being for a good purpose and given for that reason alone. They were able to look over their lives, and so saw how the intricate pattern had been woven for their ultimate good.

Those who had charge of their conduct of life on this plane, always explained that they were there only in accordance with His will. In any doubts or difficulties they asked for Divine wisdom and illumination, and it was always given.

I was present when a request was made by one of these estimable persons for an answer to a perplexing question relating to the conduct of others near the Earth. A voiceless petition was put out for guidance, and as I watched, a ray of light appeared which travelled to the petitioner. It seemed to enshroud him in a mellow ray for a short period and then disappeared. Afterwards, I was told, the answer requested had been clearly given and would be sent to those who were in need of it.

From this it will be gleaned that if the necessity arises the highest form of advice can always be obtained. The teaching of Jesus is put into practice here even if the wise-acres of the material world deem it impracticable. If man would but open himself to receive this knowledge and wisdom, then he would be more ready to carry out God's scheme for the advancement of mankind. Yet his evolution is going on, even perhaps against his knowledge, for it must be so to be in accordance with God's purpose.

The artistic tendencies of the people on this plane were very high compared with those of lower progress. They had music, painting, and art of a very high degree. Their scientists were also noteworthy. They were using all their wisdom and power to alleviate the conditions of those below them. Many were employed in an endeavour to make communications between the planes and Earth easier and more real. Others were inspiring Humans with the desire to reach forth and open the door more widely than hitherto, so that communion could take place. Some were constantly employed in giving of their knowledge to assist in uplifting the moral characters of those enduring an Earth incarnation.

Each and everyone was employed in some way in giving help to others. They asked not for thanks, those they received in the thought that they were obeying the laws of God. Man-made laws seem very mean and petty when this unselfish effort is considered.

During the space I was privileged to be on this plane, I observed that the cares of Self were entirely absent; everything was done for others, and that was the main consideration. Beside that nothing else mattered. So when you ask for angels to guard you, be assured that they will willingly do so.

52
The Temple Audience

During the period I had been engaged in my observations and studies of this planet, the companions who had been with me were also variously occupied in gaining knowledge for their purpose.

I have carefully refrained from referring to these fellow-travellers, so as to avoid confusion. But it should not be thought that what I have given you is only the fruits of my own perception. It is not so, for when we gathered together at the conclusion of our visit, we gave out the products of our travels to one another, so that we were all acquainted with the results of our joint labours.

It was by these means that we were able to support our theories by what one or another had observed, also our Conductors were always ready to enlighten or guide us on any intricate point that we had not grasped.

As a matter of fact it was the latter who supplied all the information about the higher planes. They had visited some of them on different occasions and so were well able to supplement any knowledge we had obtained, by their own personal experiences. It was an unfailing delight to them to assist us in any way possible.

The period of our visit passed very quickly, and soon I received a message to meet my fellow travellers at the dwelling of one of the Controllers of this delectable land. This message came as the usual flash of light, and I understood from it that it foreshadowed my departure.

At the appointed period I wended my way to the meeting place and greeted and was welcomed by my companions. Our Conductors were there and it was very apparent that it was a pleasant interview that lay before us.

After the arrival of the last one we were not kept waiting; our Leaders preceded us through the grounds of a large edifice, built in the shape of an old Temple similar to those of which I had seen relics in my travels on Earth. This one was in perfect condition. It appeared to be very old, but there were no signs of decay or dust about it. It was quiet, secluded, and restful, and it was easy to realise that it was used for purposes of meditation.

Following our Guides we entered, and inside found that the Temple was carved suitably to coincide with its exterior.

The resting accommodation was arranged in a half circle, with a slightly raised platform. This was ornamented by gold and subdued hues. There must have been something in the stones that caused these colours to change, for I noticed that when we first entered, the lights from them were golden and pale, but after our arrival they changed to a mixture of many harmonious tints. This was caused by the vibrations we gave out, and it had the appearance of joining up with us.

Everything in the Temple was clearly visible, yet I failed to perceive the entrance of the One who was to give us audience. I was looking at the raised platform in admiration when I noticed a stronger ray flash upwards towards the dome. I followed its flight with my eyes and then turned them back to the platform. I wondered idly why one flash had travelled further than the others, and then saw that the platform was now tenanted. A man was standing on it with upraised hands and a smile on his face. He was an impressive figure, having a firm and commanding countenance, but with wise and understanding eyes.

There was an appearance of alertness about him that indicated vivid life and a full appreciation of its potentialities. Emanating from him was an aura of a deep golden colour that expanded and contracted in a manner that was restful and encouraging. I had seen other personages with emanations, but not one so strongly emphasised as the one at whom I was now gazing. His dress was simple, a tunic with a long robe over it, and silken breeches. On his feet he wore sandal-patterned shoes.

There was no ornamentation on his dress with the exception of a loose belt with an attachment of jewels.

A silence now descended on us all as we expectantly turned towards this man He bade us welcome, and then gave thanks to God for allowing him to preside over us for a short period. At the close of his prayer he addressed us. He was obviously well acquainted with the object of our visit, and commented on the reason for it.

After this explanation, he gave us advice on the manner and way we should make use of what we had learned. I was especially interested in his remarks about giving our experiences to those now in their physical bodies. He stated that it would be found almost impossible to give the full meaning of Life to them. There were only a few advanced souls ready to receive it, and the rest could be divided into two classes: those who were sufficiently evolved to understand a small part, and the others who were so undeveloped that they would resist any knowledge of it being given to them.

The latter, however, were not to be despised because of their ignorance, but rather sympathised with for their lack of understanding. In due course these seemingly antagonistic people would have their minds opened and be eager to learn more.

It was not an easy task, he assured us, to provide proofs and convincing thoughts for the consumption of those who had no comprehension of the laws of God for His children. It had also to be remembered that a human instrument had to be used with all the failings and erratic ways pertaining to life in the physical. This provide at once a profitable channel for mistakes and errors to creep in.

Then there were the many to overcome that were only half awake, and who were in the belt that lay between the worlds. The other trouble was those who through their mistaken Earth life were now sojourning in the lower planes. These were always eager to interfere for the purpose of bringing others down to their own level.

He did not consider that we should have to deal with the Elementals, although there were humans who contacted these entities. In such a case there were those who had the necessary ways and means of quelling them when it was considers advisable. Should we, unfortunately, become involved in any contingency of this kind, we were at once to send out a message for assistance, and it would be promptly supplied.

His concluding remarks were to the effect that under all circumstances we were to be kind, considerate, and tolerant of the failings of our Earth brothers. We were not allowed to let ourselves be angered or annoyed, for we were well aware that sooner or later these people would arrive among us and ask account of our stewardship. As we, ourselves, had passed through so-called Death to Life, we should be all the more tender with them. And under no circumstances were we to give any information which could not be supported by unimpeachable proofs from our own experiences.

If questions arose that needed explicit answers outside our own knowledge then application should be made to the Temple of Knowledge, and One would arrive from there who was capable of giving the required information. We were to remember always that we would be active agents of God and served Him alone. All thanks and praise were His, and not for us.

At the end of his oration, the Speaker conversed with each of us individually cheering and encouraging us to do our work in the service of God and our fellows.

It was a heartening address, and I left more determined than ever to do my best to enlighten and help others, and to lift from the shoulders of those still walking the earth, the dread thoughts of Death, with its attendant load of misery and woe.

53
Final Notations

Later, I made a summary of the ideas and thoughts that had come to me during my visit to that advanced sphere, and concluded that the most vital thing of all was to have perfect trust in the love of God for us all, and to do whatever was in our power to serve Him and our fellow-beings. This was the only thing able to bring peace and happiness into oneself. Nothing else mattered but this. The rest was contemporary.

It was not long after this that we left the Abbey, for we had all previously notified our new friends of our speedy departure.

The return journey was similar to the previous one, with the exception that some of my fellow travellers visited the planes on which they had been invited to stay. I, myself, did not do so, as I had so much to think about, that I was determined to return to my place as soon as possible, so as to compose my thoughts on an organised basis.

My first visit after returning was to the home of the Instructor who had arranged everything for me after my studies had been completed. He was very pleased to greet me and greatly interested in the details of my travels. At the conclusion he asked me if I had made any preparations as to my future residence, and kindly suggested that I should stay with him. He thought this would be an admirable arrangement for us both, as, while he would be at the Instruction Hall he could render me any assistance I required.

I eagerly accepted his offer, and still reside with him.

It may have been noticed that I have deliberately refrained from saying anything about the reunion with my parents and friends. This was done so as not to cause a misapprehension in the minds of those who may read these writings. I did not desire to display my personal feelings about those who precede us through so-called Death.

My parents were undergoing development in the same way as we all do. They welcomed my visit, but did not evince any desire to join forces with me and return to Earth with a view to helping those left behind. They were satisfied to leave that to any who cared for such a thing, as long as they did not have to do it themselves.

There are many with similar thoughts who are pleased to remain inert as far as physical persons are concerned. Perhaps these people did not have too pleasant a time when inhabiting physical bodies and, if possible, they wished to forget that experience as far as allowed.

Others were content to await the arrival of their friends without endeavouring to make any contacts. They arrange for notification to be given to them of any expected transition of those in whom they are interested, and are then content to leave it there.

It is not everyone who is imbued with the idea of constantly visiting Earth friends. Some times it is too sorrowful, for they may not be allowed to assist, and have perhaps to watch the degradation of one they love. They are well aware that there are those who are more capable of dealing with the wants of Earth children than themselves, so leave the whole matter in their hands.

Again of course, there is a class who have to be restrained from visiting the Earth because they are so desirous of staying there. The cause of this may be briefly described as lack of development.

Also there are many who have progressed so far that they are unable to return, supposing they wished to do so, which, in their case is most unlikely.

The whole matter of descending and frequenting the Earth-plane is a well-thought-out plan by those who are wise enough to have charge of this part of God's law. It is meant that only progressive and methodic teaching shall be given to human beings who earnestly and honestly desire it, namely everything to hasten their development, and nothing to delay it.

54
My Intentions

After a period of rest and solitude during which I marshalled my facts and consolidated my knowledge, I was requested to accompany a friend who was a regular attendant to the needs of physical beings. It was conveyed to me that it was very necessary that I should be in the charge of an experienced Spirit during my first few visits in order to acquire the technique. This I thoroughly agreed was necessary, as I felt it would be of great assistance.

I fully realised also that a human Being capable of being influenced by me, must first be found before I could commence my work.

This finding of a capable person is not an easy process. It should be known that although there are a number who are endowed with the necessary qualifications, they, for some reason or the other are not ready to be used. It may be owing to the state of their minds because of wrong teaching, or that they are adverse to the idea that anyone should control their minds or bodies. It may also be that owing to their conditions in physical life they are in the dark as to the possibilities of inspiration and help from our side. There is a variety of causes for their reluctance which makes the task of selection very hard.

Many have been watched for long periods, by those on our side who have knowledge of what is required, for signs that they are willing to receive love and instruction from us. When the occasion arises, the opportunity is at once seized to impress them and urge them into the service of God and man.

The friend whom I was to accompany, possessed those who were willing to be of service, and at stated periods he visited them to give of his knowledge. He recognised a feeling of kinship between them and that he received great help from them, but admitted that it was not easy under the best of conditions to get all his messages through uncorrupted, owing to the difference between his spiritual, and their physical bodies. This obstacle had to be accepted and circumvented whenever possible, by returning to the subject and endeavouring to clear it up in that manner.

Another stone in the path was the lack of knowledge of the continuity of life by many who listened to him. It was practically impossible to convey to this type of mind what it really is and how it is carried on.

There were many, however, who tried to their utmost to understand and gain all possible information about it, and these were a joy to instruct in the laws of eternal life. This pilgrimage to the Earth life, like many other endeavours, has its compensations in joy, as well as its disappointments and sorrows.

My first return to Earth was rather bewildering, for I had, undoubtedly expected it to look the same as before, and that I, myself, should be like I had been while there. I found however, that although I seemed solid and strong, the world was dark and shadowy. The people I met were grotesque and wraithlike.

To me it was **they** who were phantoms and ghosts, whilst I was reality. Houses and walls were no impediment, they melted away before me. The whole atmosphere was dark, and caused me great distress. I knew it was daytime at the period I was there, but to me it seemed a dark and filthy night, made up of fog and mist.

Owing to my distress I was not permitted to stay very long and so quickly returned to the light and solidarity of my spirit home, I was told that the dismal feelings which occasioned my distress usually occurred at the first visit, and that after a few more experiences, the feeling would be conquered. This, later I found to be quite true for, although I can now still see and appreciate all these conditions, they do not affect me so acutely.

Yes, indeed there are many difficulties to be encountered prior to the sending of a message to those who are leading physical lives. Patience is necessary, and the knowledge that if we persevere we may be able to convince others of our continued life. This message may be believed when received, or disbelieved, but we know that its reception means that the veil between the two worlds has been imperceptibly thinned, and this in itself is sufficient reward for our efforts.

My first attempt to convince the world I had left of my continued existence was not a success; but after repeated trials I improved, and can now usually accomplish it.

At this moment I am not writing about my encounters with the world, I would rather give particulars of the New World I have entered. This has been my intention during the whole period that this book has been in preparation, and now for a space my work is nearly accomplished. I am happy in being allowed to give news of the so called Mystery of Death, and to be able to point out that we are all gainers from that supposed menace. It is God's will that we shall be eternally progressive, and so He makes provision for this by allowing us to evolve by our own efforts and in our own time. Therefore we can, with all confidence, leave the future in His hands, and know that ultimately all our needs will be satisfied.

I now leave you for a while. You, whoever you may be, endeavouring to understand a little more of the meaning of life before death intervenes; I, having received the attentions of death, striving to impress on you the fact that **there is no death**, only change. Hoping the facts of my continued existence will assist some poor faltering soul over the border-line into peace and contentment.

My last prayer is for the illumination within of all who read these writings. That when the call comes for your own transition you may have the courage of knowledge, and go forward willingly to meet God's Messenger, so cruelly and so mistakenly called Death, and thus join me in the world of constant endeavour and love.

* * *

Roundtable
Publishing Limited

Books published:
"Reborn for Love" by Hernani Guimarães Andrade
"Chico Xavier, Medium of the Century" by Guy Lyon Playfair
"Science & Spirit" by Hernani Guimarães Andrade
"The Shadows Lifted from Death" by Augustus Henry Burbidge
"Suicide, all that you need to know" by Richard Simonetti